JAMAICA

Travel Guide 2024

Your Comprehensive guide to Uncover the Island's Hidden Gems, Vibrant Culture, and Irresistible Adventures for an Unforgettable Tropical Getaway

LOWE SANDBERG

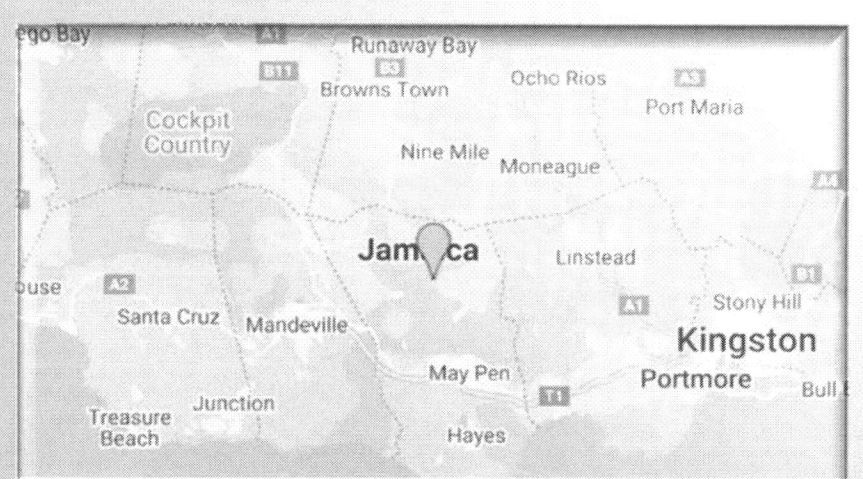

SCAN QR CODE WITH DEVICE TO VIEW MAP

Explore
JAMAICA

Copyright © 2024 by Lowe Sandberg, All rights reserved

No part of this publication may be reproduced, distributed, or transmitted in any form or by any means, including photocopying, recording, or other electronic or mechanical methods, without the prior written permission of the publisher, except in the case of brief quotations embodied in critical reviews and certain other non-commercially uses permitted by copyright law.

Table of Contents

Welcome to Jamaica 13

Why visit Jamaica? 17

15 Interesting Facts About Jamaica. 18

Chapter 1: An Overview of Jamaica 25

    History & Culture 25

    Geography and Climate 28

Chapter 2: Plan Your Trip to Jamaica 31

    16 Travel Tips You Should Know Before You Go. 31

    Best time to visit Jamaica 39

    Packing Checklist 46

    Budgeting Tips 52

Chapter 3: Getting There and Around. 57

    How to Get To Jamaica 57

    How to Get Around 64

Chapter 4: Accommodations 69

    Luxury Hotels 69

    Budget-Friendly Alternatives 74

    Bed & Breakfast 77

    Booking Tips 81

    Recommended Areas to Stay 85

    Negril 86

    Montego Bay 88

    Ocho Rios 90

    Treasure Beach 94

    Kingston 96

    Runaway Bay 98

    Port Antonio 100

    Mandeville 102

    Falmouth 104

Chapter 5: Exploring the Beauty of Jamaica. 107

Top attractions 107

Blue Hole Mineral Spring 108

Martha Brae River 109

Barney's Flower and Hummingbird Garden 109

Green Grotto Caves 110

Negril Cliffs 111

YS Falls 111

Luminous Lagoon 112

Blue and John Crow Mountains 112

Reach Falls. 113

Historical Landmarks 114

Fort Charles 115

Emancipation Park 116

Bob Marley Museum 117

Seville Great House 118

Good Hope Estate House 119

Mayfield Falls 120

Devon House 121

Chapter 6: Exploring Jamaican Beaches. **123**

Best beaches in Jamaica 123

Water Activities 128

Chapter 7: Savouring Jamaica: Culinary Experiences **135**

Must-Try Dishes in Jamaica 135

Typical Jamaican Sides 137

Popular Restaurants to Eat 138

Chapter 8: Shopping in Jamaica **147**

The greatest locations to shop in Jamaica 147

Best souvenirs to buy 153

Chapter 9: Nightlife in Jamaica **161**

Overview of nightlife scenes. 161

Popular nightclubs and clubs. 164

Live Music Venues: The Best Places to Experience Reggae .. 166

Festival and Events 170

Chapter 10: Itineraries 173

10 days in Jamaica. 173

Chapter 11: Practical Advice and Tips for Visitors 179

Local Etiquette 179

Safety and Health Tips 182

Emergency Information 185

Currency and Money Matters 188

Basic Jamaican Patois Phrases 191

Interacting with the locals. 194

Photography Tips 196

Travel Apps 200

Time Zone 204

Conclusion 206

Bonus: Travel Budget Planner & Travel Journal 209

.... 210

Welcome to Jamaica

Jamaica, the Island of Enchantment, is nestled like a diamond in the Caribbean Sea's blue embrace, south of Cuba and west of Hispaniola. Imagine turquoise oceans lapping against sugar-soft coasts, palm palms whispering to the enticing pulse of reggae sounds. Feel the warm sun kiss your skin, the aroma of exotic spices flood your senses, and a genuine grin blossom on your face, just like the Jamaican people. This, my friends, is no ordinary fantasy; it is a reality that awaits you in Jamaica...

Jamaica is more than simply a beach paradise; it's a kaleidoscope of events that will make your soul pound like a steel drum. Whether you want adventure in lush jungles, peace in secluded coves, or just wish to relax to the laid-back rhythm of "island time," this dynamic island has something to offer everyone.

Prepare to be immersed in the vivid tapestry of Jamaican life.

• Experience the island's vibrant reggae and dancehall sounds. Sway your hips at local pubs, feel the earth tremble during street parties, or just immerse yourself in the rhythm of the waves as they crash upon the coast. Jamaican music is a worldwide language, an invitation to celebrate life.

• Explore Jamaican cuisine's many tastes, including jerk chicken, ackee, and saltfish. Enjoy exquisite fish harvested directly from the crystal-clear seas, tropical fruits overflowing with sunlight, and a refreshing glass of Ting, the island's famous grapefruit soda. Each taste reflects the island's rich history and the friendliness of its inhabitants.

- Explore nature's beauty by hiking through green rainforests, swimming in waterfalls, or snorkeling in brilliant coral reefs. Climb the famed Dunn's River Falls, kayak through the stunning Luminous Lagoon, or just relax beneath the swinging shade of a palm tree on Negril's crown treasure, Seven Mile Beach. Nature in Jamaica is a soul-satisfying playground, a painting of astounding beauty.

- Embrace the spirit of "irie": Jamaicans are known for their contagious grins, welcoming attitude, and genuine kindness. Immerse yourself in local communities, learn a few words in the island's lively Patois accent, and let the "no problem" attitude wash away your concerns. In Jamaica, time slows down, and true friendships are formed through shared laughter, tales whispered on moonlight beaches, and the simple pleasure of being present.

This is just the first taste of the Jamaican Cocktail. In the next chapters, we'll go deeper into:

- We can assist you in planning your ideal Jamaican experience, including managing travel details and selecting suitable accommodations.

- Explore the island's distinct character, from Kingston's lively streets to Negril's relaxed vibe. We'll be your guide as you explore each parish's hidden jewels and local secrets.

- Creating unique experiences: From adrenaline-pumping excursions to soul-enriching retreats, we provide diverse activities to meet every traveler's preferences. Zipline over the rainforest canopy, cliff jump at Rick's Cafe, or just relax on a quiet beach - the options are infinite.

- Exploring Jamaican culture: Learn about its unique history, customs, and music. Learn about the island's vivid history, comprehend its present beat, and feel its future pulse.

Jamaica is more than simply a destination; it is a metamorphosis. It's a place where troubles melt away like snowflakes in the sun, laughing fills the air, and the rhythm of life beats to a different, more soulful melody. So pack your bags, open your heart, and prepare to experience the enchantment of Jamaica. We'll be your guide on this incredible voyage; the only difficulty you'll have is leaving a piece of yourself behind.

Welcome to paradise, Irie Mon!

Why visit Jamaica?

Plan your vacation to Jamaica for all of these reasons, among others.

Honeymoons: Jamaica is one of the world's most romantic vacation spots from the naturally heart-shaped 'jacuzzi' at Reach Falls to sunsets in Negril that will make you fall in love.

Weddings: There is no finer location to get married than here. There are several ways to rest, relax, and enjoy your time in Jamaica before, during, and after saying your "I do's."

Nature: Discover why Errol Flynn and numerous others declare Jamaica the most beautiful spot they've ever seen. Majestic waterfalls, vast rivers, and lush landscapes are just the start of the adventure.

History: As one of the world's most diversified countries, visiting Jamaica is an exciting learning experience.

Adventure: The island of rhythm and sway is also the home of adventure. Come discover our favorite destinations.

Food: Jamaica is a gourmet attraction with jerks, patties, and world-famous ice cream.

Beaches: Claim your position on our lovely beaches. Jamaica has a beach for everyone, whether you want to explore the underwater world or just relax in the sun.

Entertainment: Jamaica is the Caribbean's cultural hub. Visit us to enjoy live reggae music, street dances, festivals, carnivals, and more.

Weather: Warm Caribbean weather with occasional liquid sunlight makes for a fun vacation.

The People: When you arrive, you will be greeted by some of the world's nicest people. Say hello and speak with us! Don't worry; we'll teach you some of our dialect patois.

15 Interesting Facts About Jamaica.

Did you know Jamaica was the home of reggae music? Or that Jamaica's seas contain the world's second-largest coral reef system?

These are just a handful of the intriguing facts about this fascinating nation. Continue reading to discover more.

Jamaica has a year-round tropical climate.

The island has a Caribbean climate that is pleasant and sunny all year. June through November are the "cooler" months for guests who like to swim in water that isn't as warm as bathwater.

It's due to the gentle trade breezes. If you're planning a vacation during these months, bring lots of sunscreen—the rays may be powerful!

Jamaica is the home of Reggae music.

Bob Marley, one of history's most renowned and influential artists, was born in this stunning island country. Reggae music's characteristic Caribbean rhythms and melodies may be heard across Jamaica. While you are there, stop by a local recording studio.

Jamaica's mountains are so old that they contain fossils from prehistoric times.

The island's highest peak is Blue Mountain Peak. It rises 7,402 feet (approximately 2,100 meters) above sea level. You'll feel like you're on top of the world as you take in the panoramic views of these great heights.

The world's second-largest coral reef system is in Jamaican waters.

The coral reef in Jamaica is more than 120 miles long and home to various gorgeous aquatic species. The reefs are home to colorful fish, sharks, sea turtles, stingrays, dolphins, and other marine life.

Also, visit one of Jamaica's many gorgeous beaches and discover the magnificent underwater ecology. You'll surely enjoy all the splendor that awaits you in the depths below.

Jamaica was the first British colony to achieve independence from Great Britain.

On August 6, 1962, this 32-mile island republic finally achieved independence. Jamaicans commemorate Independence Day yearly with parades and festivities around the island. It's a celebration of their hard-earned independence.

Jamaica has a population of about 3 million people who live in an area approximately twice the size of Rhode Island. This island nation has the third largest English-speaking population in the Americas. Nonetheless, it expands year after year. With so many people living here, there is always something intriguing happening!

Jamaica has some very breathtaking beaches.

From Negril's 7-mile length of gorgeous sand to Montego Bay's white sandy coastlines, there are innumerable lovely beaches along this amazing country's coast. Jamaica is an excellent place to enjoy the sun and surf.

Jamaica is the birthplace of fast runners, including Usain Bolt, the fastest man in history, and Asafa Powell, the world record holder in the 100-meter sprint. Jamaica has a long and impressive history of producing world-class athletes. So, attend any of Jamaica's sporting events—you'll undoubtedly witness someone extraordinary!

Jamaica was formerly home to Captain Morgan, a famous pirate.

Captain Henry Morgan was a buccaneer who patrolled the Spanish Main between the 1660s and 1770s. His favorite refuge on dry land? That'd be Port Royal in Kingston Harbor! While in Jamaica, you may also see Port Royal Island.

The colors of the Jamaican flag are unique.

Jamaica's flag is black, green, and gold, a unique combination seen only in this country. Each of these hues has a significance, making them even more unique. The flag's three hues represent obstacles, sunshine, and agriculture.

Jamaica's island produces more than 200 exotic and delicious fruits.

This nation boasts an abundance of wonderful fruits, ranging from mangos to star apples. If you're a foodie, explore the local markets. While you're there, try some of these delicious delicacies! You will not regret it.

Jamaica has several bustling cities, such as Kingston, Portmore, and Mandeville.

Jamaica is a diversified nation with many people, locations, and activities to offer. From busy metropolises to peaceful towns like Treasure Beach and Black River Town, the island kingdom has something for everyone.

Jamaica cultivates one of the world's rarest and most expensive coffees

Blue Mountain coffee is cultivated only in Jamaica's lush soil. With such an incredible scent and flavor, it's no surprise that coffee enthusiasts worldwide treasure this brew.

Jamaica is home to the world's only Blue Lager.

Blue Mountain Lager is a light, pleasant beer. It is made with pure spring water sourced from Jamaica's highlands. If you're searching for something unusual, try this when visiting Jamaica.

The people of Jamaica have a good sense of style.

Jamaicans know how to create a unique fashion statement. From their vibrant and eccentric attire to their strikingly gorgeous jewelry. If you need ideas for your next outfit, visit the neighborhood stores.

Bring It All Together

Jamaica's stunning nature makes it an ideal holiday destination. This lovely island country has stunning beaches and a thriving music scene.

Chapter 1: An Overview of Jamaica

History & Culture

Jamaica has a rich history due to the numerous immigrants who have moved here throughout the years, and it has also amassed an incredible collection of historical buildings from the major colonial powers of Spain and Britain. Jamaican culture is most witnessed during festivals, when there is street dancing and funky music, although the residents are relaxed and enjoy Rasta life all year round.

History

The Arawak Indians arrived on the island before Christopher Columbus in 1494, but nothing of their civilization survived. The Spanish claimed Jamaica first and lingered there for a century and a half until being evicted by the British in the mid-1600s.

Spanish Town, located west of Kingston, is home to some of Jamaica's oldest landmarks. Saint James Cathedral, located near the Old King's House, was erected on a demolished Spanish chapel site and is now the oldest Anglican church outside of the United Kingdom.

They also built a fort at Kingston Harbor (Port Royal) to guard against a potential Spanish assault, which drew seafarers, pirates, and prostitutes, transforming the area into a commercial hub. An earthquake in 1692 and a storm in 1722 devastated the town, which was abandoned in favor of the growing Kingston. Parts of the ancient town are still popular tourist destinations.

Jamaica would become the greatest slave colony in the Caribbean as the British established enormous plantations in the lush interior and brought in waves of West Africans to labor them. The island developed early, despite numerous clashes with rebellious slaves, who were finally freed in 1838.

Rose Hall is the most well-known plantation. Built-in 1770, it was one of the biggest and is now a significant historical landmark, thought to be haunted by the famed White Witch Annie. In Montego Bay, the Milk River Baths, near Doctors Cave, were also built about this period in 1794 when an escaped plantation worker found its medicinal waters.

Jamaica suffered economically and due to natural calamities throughout the 1900s, but political upheaval was on the horizon for the now-majority black population. Exports expanded to include bananas, minerals, and other commodities, and the country proclaimed independence from Britain in 1962. Jamaica's most renowned son, Bob Marley, dies twenty years later. His previous home in Kingston is now a museum and one of the most famous tourist attractions.

Throughout the 1970s and 1980s, Jamaican politics was controlled by two opposing white politicians supported by violent slum gangs that often fought. Each took turns leading, but it was Michael Manley's socialist beliefs that alienated the US and exacerbated the country's economic misery.

Jamaica has recently been plagued with political irregularities, and the movement to establish a republic to succeed Queen Elizabeth II as head of state may be on the horizon. The tourism business is prospering, and the country's athletes' repeated success at the Olympic Games (particularly superstar Usain Bolt) elevates the country worldwide.

Culture

Jamaicans are generally warm and welcoming, with influences from Africa and the Caribbean. As a very religious people, the island is overflowing with churches, with a Protestant majority alongside Catholic, Jewish, and Muslim religions, as well as the cult of Rastafarianism.

It is a casual and carefree lifestyle away from the hectic metropolis, with frequent dancing and marching in the streets for various occasions. The pounding of steel drums, soca, and reggae music are everywhere, and culture can also be observed in the arts and crafts produced at crowded marketplaces around the island.

Ganja smoking (while illegal) is similarly essential for many residents, and life is a beach, particularly in Montego Bay. The abundance of locally sourced seafood, jerk chicken, and Jamaican rum is unforgettable. Although informal, more formal attire is required at the premium, all-inclusive beachside hotels.

Geography and Climate

Geography

Jamaica is 140 kilometers (87 miles) south of Cuba and 190 kilometers (118 miles) west of Haiti. Jamaica's length may reach 235 kilometers (146 miles), while its breadth ranges from 34 to 84 kilometers (21 to 52 miles). Jamaica has an area of 10,992 km² (4,244 sq mi). On the other hand, Jamaica is the biggest island in the Caribbean Commonwealth and the third largest in the Greater Antilles, behind only Cuba and Hispaniola. Several tiny islands are off Jamaica's southern coast, notably Port Royal Cays. Pedro Bank, located southwest of mainland Jamaica, is a shallow sea region with several cays (low islands or reefs) that stretches 160 kilometers (99 miles) from east to west. Morant Bank, home to Morant Cays, is located 51 kilometers (32 miles) southeast of Morant Point, the easternmost point on the Jamaican mainland. Alice Shoal is located 260 kilometers (160 miles) southwest of Jamaica's main island and is part of the Jamaican-Colombian joint system. The exclusive economic zone covers 258,137 kilometers (99,667 square miles).

Climate

Jamaica has two kinds of climates. A high-altitude tropical climate prevails on the mountain's windward side, whereas a semi-arid environment dominates the leeward side. Warm trade winds from the east and northeast deliver rains all year. Rainfall is the heaviest from May to October, with maximum rainfall occurring throughout these two months. The average annual precipitation is 1,960 millimeters (77.2 inches). However, precipitation is much greater in mountainous places facing north and east. In the top altitudes of the John Crow and Blue Mountains, when moist winds bring rain, precipitation surpasses 5,080 millimeters (200 inches) every year. The southwestern part of the island lies under the rain shadow of the mountains, resulting in a semi-arid environment with annual rainfall of less than 760 millimeters (29.9 inches). Jamaica's temperatures are consistent throughout the year, ranging from 23.5 to 30 degrees. C (74.3 to 86.0 °F) in the lowlands and 15 to 22 °C (59.0 to 71.6 °F) in the highlands. Temperatures at the Blue Mountains' summit may dip to 10 °C (50 °F). In addition to northeasterly trade winds, the island receives pleasant onshore breezes during the day and chilly offshore winds at night. These are known in Jamaica as "Doctor

Breeze" and "Undertaker's Breeze," respectively. Jamaica is positioned in the Atlantic Ocean's storm belt.

As a consequence, the island periodically suffers severe hurricane damage. Hurricane Charlie in 1951 and Hurricane Gilbert in 1988 were two powerful storms that slammed the island, causing death and devastation. Several additional major storms passed near the island, causing damage. For example, Hurricane Allen wiped out the entire Jamaican banana harvest in 1980. Hurricane Ivan (2004) struck the island, inflicting major damage and several fatalities. Hurricanes Dennis and Emily deluged the island with rain in 2005. storm Dean, a Category 4 storm, killed many people and caused major damage in Jamaica in August 2007. The first known storm to impact Jamaica occurred in 1519. Tropical cyclones have often affected the island. The two coldest periods in the last 250 years (the 1780s and 1810s) witnessed an exceptionally high number of hurricanes in Jamaica. Another surge of activity occurred during the 1910s, the coldest decade of the twentieth century. On the other side, storm incidence declined dramatically between 1968 and 1994, coinciding with the Great Sahel Drought.

Chapter 2: Plan Your Trip to Jamaica

16 Travel Tips You Should Know Before You Go.

Aside from pulsating reggae and dancehall tunes, Jamaica's natural beauty, including magnificent beaches, jungle-covered mountains, tropical waterfalls, and its world-renowned culinary industry, distinguishes it from other Caribbean islands.

Learning the country's unstated customs and etiquette can help you understand what makes Jamaica so special and address any travel worries. Here's everything I believe you should know before you go.

Make sensible choices on where to stay.

Jamaica is one of the Caribbean's biggest islands, so where you stay will depend on your preferences. Negril and the north coast provide the greatest beaches and water activities.

Montego Bay and Ocho Rios provide good food options and are close to natural wonders and vibrant nightlife, but Kingston, the capital, reigns supreme in the Jamaican music scene.

Treasure Beach (south coast) and Port Antonio (north coast) provide a taste of low-key, laid-back Jamaica, while Charles Town (northeast coast) offers a glimpse into traditional Maroon culture.

Hiking up Blue Mountain Peak and hiking across rural Cockpit Country are best planned from Kingston or Falmouth, respectively.

Bring a mosquito net, just in case.

Jamaican mosquitos do not transmit malaria, although there are periodic outbreaks of dengue illness. Some guesthouses and hotels do not supply mosquito netting, so carry your own.

Avon Skin So Soft is the greatest repellent for no-see-ums (midges), small biting insects that reside near water and cause highly irritating bites.

It is feasible to visit without renting a vehicle.

A mix of luxury, air-conditioned buses, packed minibusses, and taxis services the principal towns of Jamaica.

It is perfectly feasible to travel across Jamaica using public transit but to reach more isolated locations; you will need plenty of time and patience or your vehicle. If you're planning a road vacation, automobile rentals are accessible at Kingston and Montego Bay airports.

Carry some Jamaican dollars.

Credit cards are virtually always accepted in upscale hotels, stores, and restaurants. Cash (Jamaican dollars) reigns supreme elsewhere in Jamaica, while US dollars will suffice in most tourist areas.

ATMs and currency exchanges are available in Montego Bay, Kingston, and Ocho Rios. However, currency exchanges (cambios) provide the greatest prices. Airport rates are not very low, and you will be charged an ATM fee if you withdraw cash. Small changes are ideal for purchasing from street sellers and using public transportation.

You may travel throughout the storm season.

Jamaica is susceptible to hurricanes throughout the Atlantic hurricane season (early June to late November); most storms hit between August and October. Following a few simple criteria, you may plan your travel to Jamaica during hurricane season.

- ❖ Obtain travel insurance that includes storm coverage.
- ❖ Download a hurricane-tracking app.
- ❖ As soon as possible, decide whether to attempt to get an early flight home (which may be expensive/difficult) or bunker down throughout a storm.

- ❖ Check whether your hotel/guesthouse has a storm shelter and is prone to floods or landslides. Hotels with private generators are less likely to have power disruptions.
- ❖ Prepare emergency supplies such as a flashlight, first aid kit, food, and water.
- ❖ Comply with evacuation instructions.
- ❖ Relocate closer to the Kingston or Montego Bay airport for easy access and evacuation during hurricanes.
- ❖ If a storm hits Jamaica, be patient and plan to prolong your vacation.

Feel free to let loose on a night out.

Casual summer clothes are appropriate for most situations. However, certain premium resorts and expensive restaurants need smart casual attire.

Women often wear "batty riders" (skin-tight shorts) and equally figure-hugging tops to Kingston and Montego Bay nightclubs, while males often wear jeans and shirts. Remember, the atmosphere is relaxed and nonjudgmental, so looking or judging is inappropriate.

If you want a more relaxed and low-key look, dress accordingly. It's a party, after all.

This might be a genuine eye-opener if you're new to the dancehall scene. The dancing may be provocative, as locals compete by "whining" - gyrating their hips and waists to the music.

You'll likely be pulled into the brawl, and then it's sink or swim time! If you give the dancing your all, you'll receive positive feedback from regulars, who could even volunteer to teach you how to dance.

Stay awake for the nightlife.

Jamaica never sleeps. That is at least true for Kingston, Negril, Montego Bay, and Ocho Rios. Negril is ideal for beach parties, while Kingston boasts the slickest nightclubs, music events, and street dances.

Things seldom start before midnight, and revelers celebrate until daybreak. Overnight reggae and dancehall performances include at least a dozen musicians, with the crowd showing their excitement with "bullet bullet" chants and two-finger gun salutes. It's noisy but usually in good humor.

Do speak to strangers.

Unlike many other major cities, where starting discussions with strangers is frowned upon, Jamaica is the polar opposite.

Some Jamaicans may approach you hoping to conduct business (see "How to handle hustling and harassment"). Nonetheless, many people are genuinely interested in knowing more about you and find standoffish behavior insulting. You'll find yourself repeating "good morning," "good afternoon," and "good night" (both as greetings and farewells) often.

Elders are treated with particular respect. An exchange of polite chat with merchants attempting to sell you fruit or trinkets is much superior to coldly dismissing folks just trying to earn a life.

Respect Rastafarianism.

Around 1% of Jamaicans practice Rastafarianism, a religious and political movement that combines Biblical teachings with viewing Ethiopia as the Promised Land, using ganja to commune with Jah (God), and living a "natural" lifestyle involving I-tal food (free of artificial additives) and the growth of locs and beards for men.

Some Rastafarians live in tiny, isolated, self-sufficient communities; others may only come if they first contact the elders to seek permission. The Rastafari Indigenous Village beyond Montego Bay provides a more accessible (and touristic) experience.

Is negotiating acceptable?

Gentle bargaining is typical and expected when purchasing items from individual vendors or shopping in rural marketplaces. Otherwise, you are required to pay the indicated charge. As usual, be mindful that this is someone's livelihood, and if you're not satisfied with the price, go away with a smile.

Is Jamaica an LGBTIQ+-friendly country?

Jamaican culture is primarily homophobic, and the homosexual community in Kingston is firmly underground, with public demonstrations of love between gay couples strictly discouraged. Sexual actions between males are prohibited and punishable by up to ten years in jail.

However, in prominent tourist areas, hotels (including some all-inclusive) accept LGBTIQ+ guests.

What You Need to Know About Public Bathrooms

Shopping malls, cafés, and restaurants charge for using their facilities, which may not usually satisfy basic sanitary requirements, and woe betide you if you need a restroom outside the hospitality industry.

Is Jamaican tap water drinkable?

Most of Jamaica's tap water is safe to drink. Avoid tap water in remote rural locations, and avoid ice sold on the street as "belly wash," "snowcones," or "sky juice" (shaved-ice cones sweetened with fruit juice).

While bottled water is easily accessible, recycling plastic is a concern, so carry reusable flasks.

Is Jamaica a vegetarian or vegan-friendly destination?

Plant-based I-tal ("vital") cuisine, a key principle of Rastafarianism, is abundantly accessible and tasty.

Expect freshly squeezed fruit juices, plantain fritters, steaming callaloo (Jamaica's equivalent of spinach), tropical fruit, and much more. Rice 'n' peas (rice with kidney beans) are non-Rasta restaurants' most popular side dish.

How to deal with hustling and harassment.

Travelers will likely experience constant sales pitches from hustlers, especially in the main tourist destinations of Montego Bay, Negril, and Ocho Rios.

Some may be extremely persistent in hoping you would purchase whatever they offer, only to be left alone and refuse politely but firmly.

Common Scams and How to Avoid Them

Common scams include young guys transporting to a prominent tourist destination (such as a waterfall or swimming hole) and claiming that you only paid for one trip.

Self-appointed "guides" may offer numerous add-ons after excursions, so be sure you understand what the agreed-upon charge includes before accepting their services.

Best time to visit Jamaica

With its stunning beaches, lush tropical woods, and some of the top resorts in the Caribbean, Jamaica has long tempted winter-weary tourists eager to recharge under the sun. However, there is much more for guests to enjoy in this Caribbean paradise.

"The winter season was once the time of the year when travelers would flock to the Caribbean to escape the cold – but that's not the case anymore," explains Kenton Jones, managing director at the magnificent and exclusive 91-villa Tryall Club in Montego Bay. "Jamaica has become a year-round destination for travel."

Here's an overview of Jamaica's primary travel seasons:

- ❖ High season: December - April.
- ❖ Shoulder seasons: May, June, October, and November.
- ❖ Low season: July-September.

Discover the ideal times to visit Jamaica for stunning beaches and must-see events like the island's pulsating Carnival festivities and the world-famous Reggae Sumfest.

Best times to visit with less crowds

While Jamaica has enough to offer all year, the crowds are at their fewest "when the weather is nicest 'back home,'" says Houston Moncure. Moncure, managing director of the exclusive Bluefields Bay Villas on Jamaica's peaceful and radiant southwestern coast, attests that this is a portion of the island that never seems crowded, even though cruise ships and bustling all-inclusive bring thousands of people elsewhere.

Enjoy reduced crowds around the island starting at the end of April, with visitor numbers decreasing even more until Thanksgiving when a flood of US-based vacationers arrives. "Traveling during [these months] has its perks since people can enjoy less traffic as you travel from destination to destination as well as fewer crowds in town centers, public beaches, and restaurants," according to Jones.

Island sources also mention a short but noticeable dip in January. "Festive season travelers head home, and most people wind down from the holidays," according to Moncure. "You'll generally see a drop in holiday season prices, accompanied by gorgeous, cloudless weather."

Best Time to Visit for Good Weather

Jamaica has the greatest weather from December to March when even passing showers are unusual. Warm Caribbean temperatures are typical, with lower humidity than the rest of the year. This lovely weather makes December through April the ideal time to enjoy languid days on some of Jamaica's loveliest beaches.

While rain begins to fall in late April or May and may linger until early November, "remember that these rain storms tend to last for just an hour or two during the afternoons, as is customary throughout most of the Caribbean," notes Moncure. "It's the perfect excuse to disconnect for a few hours and nap in a hammock among the lush landscape."

Best times to visit with less crowds

While Jamaica has enough to offer all year, the crowds are at their fewest "when the weather is nicest 'back home,'" says Houston Moncure. Moncure, managing director of the exclusive Bluefields Bay Villas on Jamaica's peaceful and radiant southwestern coast, attests that this is a portion of the island that never seems crowded, even though cruise ships and bustling all-inclusive bring thousands of people elsewhere.

Enjoy reduced crowds around the island starting at the end of April, with visitor numbers decreasing even more until Thanksgiving when a flood of US-based vacationers arrives. "Traveling during [these months] has its perks since people can enjoy less traffic as you travel from destination to destination as well as fewer crowds in town centers, public beaches, and restaurants," according to Jones.

Island sources also mention a short but noticeable dip in January. "Festive season travelers head home, and most people wind down from the holidays," according to Moncure. "You'll generally see a drop in holiday season prices, accompanied by gorgeous, cloudless weather."

Best Time to Visit for Good Weather

Jamaica has the greatest weather from December to March when even passing showers are unusual. Warm Caribbean temperatures are typical, with lower humidity than the rest of the year. This lovely weather makes December through April the ideal time to enjoy languid days on some of Jamaica's loveliest beaches.

While rain begins to fall in late April or May and may linger until early November, "remember that these rain storms tend to last for just an hour or two during the afternoons, as is customary throughout most of the Caribbean," notes Moncure. "It's the perfect excuse to disconnect for a few hours and nap in a hammock among the lush landscape."

Best Time to Visit for Lower Prices

Jamaica has many hotels, from low-cost guesthouses and all-inclusive resorts to some of the most abundant in the Caribbean. Those hoping to save money on everything from lodging to activities and excursions should schedule their holiday between May and early November when costs are lower overall.

May-June and October-November shoulder seasons may result in considerable discounts for discerning visitors. However, rates will normally fall in July and September, when traveler numbers are at their lowest.

For tourists seeking to escape the chilly weather back home, the early weeks of January often witness a drop in lodging costs after the conclusion of the Christmas season. Prices often rise again in early February as tourist numbers increase.

The Best Time to Visit for Carnival

Visit Jamaica in early April for one of the island's most important celebrations: Carnival. While Trinidad and Tobago are well-known for their Carnival festivities, Jamaica's version is a vibrant swirl of music, dancing, and cuisine fueled by soca and calypso sounds.

"Throughout Carnival, there are fetes, beach parties, and smaller street parades, which all lead up to the biggest event of Carnival: the National Carnival Road March in Kingston. The Road March is a masquerade parade where the whole island comes together in celebration, dancing throughout the streets in the most incredible costumes while mas bands play the music that is part of Jamaica's cultural identity," said Jones.

While the festival used to be nearly entirely focused on Kingston, it has since spread to other areas of the island, including Ochos Rios, Montego Bay, and Negril.

Best Time to Visit for Reggae

Jamaica's most identifiable cultural product has long been a popular tourist attraction. It's difficult to avoid the irresistible sounds of reggae in Jamaica at any time of year. However, music fans know that the island's annual Reggae Sumfest, held in Montego Bay in July, is unquestionably the greatest time to visit Jamaica for a full immersion in the rhythm — and the culture.

This year marked the 30th anniversary of Sumfest, Jamaica's premier reggae festival. "This week-long celebration has been the biggest festival in the Caribbean and one that invites visitors to dance from dawn till dusk to a lineup of the hottest dancehall artists, the biggest names in reggae, and top international talent while also experiencing all that Montego Bay has to offer," said Jones.

International stars who cross genres tend to bring large audiences but don't miss out on the smaller local performers. Montego Bay's resorts and hotels, such as The Tryall Club, are the ideal places to stay if you want to be right in the action, but be sure you book ahead of time.

Best Time to Visit for Island Adventures.

From July to late October, the wetter months are ideal for adventurous trips away from the beach and into the island's interior.

During these months, river rafting and tubing become more adventurous due to bigger watersheds, but the landscape blossoms brilliant green and is more magnificent than ever. Similarly, waterfalls will be at their most breathtaking. Hiking routes that traverse the island may be a little more difficult after rain, but beautiful woodlands make for appealing expeditions. During the rainy season, the island's magnificent Blue Lagoon stands out against tropical coastlines brimming with activity.

Alternatively, the bioluminescent Luscious Lagoon on the island's north coast near Falmouth is most active during the dry months of the year, from December to April. The dazzling blue bioluminescence visible to nocturnal visitors is even more striking against the darkness of a new moon.

Worst Time to Visit

Travelers should remember that Jamaica is located inside the Atlantic storm belt. The hurricane season lasts from the beginning of June to the end of November. However, the peak of tropical activity in the area is usually between mid-August and mid-October.

However, there is no awful time to visit Jamaica. The island is verdant and lush even during the rainy season, making the occasional afternoon rains seem worthwhile. When you consider the reduced rates and fewer crowds during these months, it's clear why Jamaica is becoming a more popular destination, even during the traditionally low season.

Packing Checklist

A brief introduction on what to carry for Jamaica.

To go to Jamaica, you must arrange numerous things ahead of time. To begin, you must have a passport that is still valid for at least six months. You may also need a visa depending on your nationality, so verify the entrance requirements before you go. Having enough travel insurance to cover medical emergencies and trip cancellations is also critical. In terms of health, it is suggested that you be vaccinated against hepatitis A and B and typhoid, particularly if you intend to visit rural regions. Finally, pack proper clothes and footwear for the tropical temperature, sunscreen, and bug repellent.

Here are some items you should consider packing:

Lightweight and breathable clothes

Pack comfortable and lightweight clothes made from breathable materials such as cotton or linen. Jamaica has a tropical climate, which means it may become hot and humid.

Swimwear

Jamaica is famed for its stunning beaches, so bring a swimsuit.

Sunscreen and sunglasses.

Wear high-SPF sunscreen and eyewear to protect yourself from the sun's rays.

Insect repellent

Mosquitoes and other insects might be an issue, particularly during the rainy season, so bring bug repellant.

Comfortable footwear

Pack comfy shoes or sandals to use when walking or trekking.

Travel adapter

Jamaica has the same electrical outlets as the United States and Canada, so you may require a travel adaptor if you're visiting from another location.

Medications

If you are taking any prescriptions, carry enough for the whole trip.

Travel documentation

Bring your passport, visa (if required), travel insurance, and other necessary documentation.

What to Pack for Jamaica When Entering Jamaica

Valid passport.

You will need a passport that is valid for at least six months.

Visa (if applicable)

Depending on your nationality, you may need a visa to visit Jamaica. Check the admission criteria for your particular nation ahead of time.

Custom Declaration Form

Upon arrival, you must fill out and submit a customs declaration form.

Proof of onward travel.

Immigration officers may want documentation of further travel, such as a return ticket or a ticket to another place.

Cash

You may be required to pay a departure tax when departing Jamaica, so be prepared with cash.

Travel insurance

You should obtain travel insurance to cover any medical emergency or cancellations.

What to Pack for Jamaica for a Better Trip (Personal)

Sunscreen

Jamaica is a sunny vacation, so bring lots of sunscreen to protect your skin from the intense tropical sun.

Insect repellent

Mosquitoes and other insects may be a nuisance in Jamaica, so pack bug repellent to keep them away.

Swimsuit

Jamaica's beautiful beaches and warm Caribbean seas make it an ideal destination to swim and sunbathe.

Comfortable walking shoes.

If you want to tour Jamaica's natural beauty or historical places, you need comfortable walking shoes to keep your feet happy.

Lightweight clothes

Jamaica's environment is often warm and humid, so bring light, breathable clothes to remain cool and comfortable.

Travel adapter

Jamaica has the same electrical outlets as the United States, so if you're traveling from another nation with a different plug, carry a travel adaptor to charge your electronics.

Personal medicines

If you have prescription drugs or other vital medical goods, keep them in your carry-on baggage.

What kind of clothing do you carry for Jamaica?

Lightweight, breathable clothes.

Jamaica has a warm, tropical environment, so bring lightweight, breathable clothes made of natural fibers such as cotton, linen, or rayon to keep cool and comfortable.

Swimwear

Bring a swimsuit or two, whether you're going to the beach, a pool, or a waterfall.

Comfortable walking shoes

If you want to visit Jamaica's natural beauty or historic places, pack comfortable walking shoes or sandals with decent grip.

Cover-ups or wraps.

If you want to visit religious sites or other places requiring modest attire, pack a lightweight cover-up or wrap to put over your clothes.

Rain gear

Jamaica may have tropical rains, particularly during the rainy season, so pack a lightweight rain jacket or poncho.

Dressier clothes

If you want to eat at a fine restaurant or attend a special function, carry dressier attire, such as a sundress or collared shirt.

Mosquito-repellent clothes

Mosquitoes may be a nuisance in Jamaica, particularly during certain times of the year, so carry mosquito-repellent clothes or spray.

Budgeting Tips

Jamaica is often regarded as one of the most popular tropical holiday locations. However, first-time visitors to the Caribbean are generally hesitant to come due to the high expense. So, in this area, you'll discover how to enjoy Jamaica on a budget. Visit Things to Do in Jamaica and save money with these seven ideas and strategies.

Traveling to Jamaica isn't as pricey as you would imagine. At the present currency rate, a trip to the island nation may cost as little as $200. Once there, you can obtain decent lodging for roughly $48 per night. Getting around is also affordable, with a bus journey costing about $1.

A delicious supper would cost you roughly $11. Depending on the activities you wish to check out, you may have to pay roughly $79 each.

How to Save on Your Jamaica Trip

Nevertheless, you may still reduce the expense of your Jamaican holiday. Here are some helpful recommendations for visiting Jamaica and saving money:

Choose the appropriate season to visit.

Winter and spring are frequently the busiest seasons in Jamaica, with many visitors visiting. This is also when hotel costs may skyrocket, and reservations sell out quickly. Summer and autumn, on the other hand, are peak seasons for resort discounts. If you still want to travel during the busy season, book early so that costs do not increase.

Book a cruise!

This may seem like unusual advice since cruises are frequently regarded to be solely for the wealthy. However, cruises may help you save money on your vacation since they include transportation, lodgings, and even activities in one package. You may skip the airfare ticket since some cruises have local home ports where you can just drive to and join the ship.

Consider the exchange rate.

Many first-time tourists overlook this fact. Exchange rates may impact practically every aspect of your travel. Fortunately,

Jamaica's currency rate is linked to the US dollar rate, so you won't have to worry about abrupt swings in value. However, it is advisable to watch currency fluctuations to decide how much cash to carry.

Discard the exchange counter.

As previously said, most places in Jamaica take US dollars as a form of payment, so you won't have to worry about exchange rates. On the other hand, if you need to pay in Jamaican dollars, it is preferable to withdraw cash from ATMs rather than visit currency exchange counters. This is because the former utilizes the international exchange rate, often better than the latter's.

Find where the locals eat.

Not only can you find cheaper meals here, but you can also sample more authentic local food. If you are unclear about where to locate these restaurants, you can always ask the hotel front desk or local taxi drivers to take you there.

Visit your local food store.

Why not prepare your own instead of heading to the hotel restaurant or cafeteria for a snack? Jamaica boasts a robust network of grocery shops and marketplaces where you can acquire anything from bread to fresh fruits, seafood, and other necessities. These will come in useful if you have a midnight hunger.

Forget about the resort!

Depending on your plans, you may not even use the facilities supplied. So, get a hotel with fewer accommodations instead of paying for them. You also shouldn't be too picky about your location. While your hotel may be farther from the beach, you can still swim there at a lower fee than tight beachfront resorts.

Chapter 3: Getting There and Around.

How to Get To Jamaica

Jamaica, one of the Caribbean's most popular tourist destinations and a regional transportation center, is well-serviced by direct flights from North America, the United Kingdom, and other European countries. Most guests purchase packages that include flights, lodging, and airport transfers. However, there are also fantastic flight-only prices available. Most airlines fly into Montego Bay, with some also landing in Kingston, which is more handy if traveling to Port Antonio or the Blue Mountains.

By Air.

Airfares are usually seasonal, with the greatest rates between December and mid-January, when the weather is at its finest, and during the summer school vacations (July to early September). Fares fall during the "shoulder" seasons, which run from November and mid-January to April (except Easter), while the low season, which runs from May, June, and mid-September to November, offers the greatest pricing.

Flights from the UK and Ireland

Air Jamaica, British Airways, and Virgin provide direct flights from London Gatwick to Montego Bay and Kingston (9 hours). The average high/low season scheduled prices are £950/750, although exceptional bargains may bring fares as low as £450. Caribbean specialized agencies, like Newmont Travel, are your best choice for bargains with these flights since they often offer lower tickets than the airlines themselves.

Booking a charter trip may save money, with an average rate of roughly £500 and rare bargains as low as £300; charter carriers' flight and hotel packages often provide significant savings. Charter operators operating flights to Montego Bay include First Choice from Gatwick, Birmingham, and Manchester, Thomas Cook from Gatwick and Manchester, and Thomson from Gatwick.

Because there are no direct flights from Ireland to Jamaica, the most convenient route is to fly to the United Kingdom and then take a direct flight there.

Flights from the United States and Canada

Because all-inclusive package trips are so popular, most travelers to Jamaica fly on charter airlines. However, there are several daily direct flights from various regions of the United States. However, Canada is not well-serviced.

Flying time from the United States varies greatly. The trip from Miami to Montego Bay takes just 1 hour 25 minutes, making it the primary US departure point for Jamaica, while the travel from New York takes 3 hours 20 minutes. Caribbean Airlines, which took over Air Jamaica in 2010 and is now the country's national airline, has a large schedule of direct flights to Montego Bay and Kingston from Fort Lauderdale (1hr 43min), Orlando (2hr), New York (3hr 20min), and Toronto (4hr). Their high- and low-season flights to Montego Bay average US$600/300 (including taxes), with particularly attractive special bargains available during summer.

In addition, a handful of low-cost airlines provide very competitive prices. Spirit offers no-frills round-trip flights from Fort Lauderdale to Montego Bay and Kingston starting at only US$99, including taxes. Jet Blue flies from New York to Montego Bay and Kingston for $230, including taxes, with connections from several US locations, including Los Angeles, Phoenix, and Chicago. Other US airlines offer direct flights to Jamaica, including American Airlines from Miami to Kingston, United from Houston and New York to

Montego Bay and Kingston, Delta from Atlanta and New York to Kingston, as well as from Atlanta, New York, Memphis, Detroit, Washington, Minneapolis, and Los Angeles to Montego Bay, and US Airways from Boston, Charlotte, and Philadelphia.

From Canada, WestJet and Air Canada (aircanaada.com) provide direct flights from Toronto to Kingston and Montego Bay (both around 4 hours); high/low season rates cost Can$900/500. If traveling from another area of Canada, you must first fly to Toronto or a regional hub in the United States before connecting to Jamaica.

Flights between Australia and New Zealand

There are no direct flights from Australia or New Zealand to Jamaica; instead, go to the United States, the United Kingdom, or Europe (Italy or the Netherlands) and then take an onward connection. The cheapest and most easy way is via Los Angeles. Expect to spend roughly NZ$1820 from Auckland and Aus$1920 from Sydney to go to Jamaica, with an average flight duration of around 44 hours.

By the Sea

Cruise ships

Cruising is one of the most popular methods of going to Jamaica by water. Jamaica is a popular cruise line destination, and major ports such as Ocho Rios, Falmouth, and Montego Bay often welcome these floating cities.

- ❖ Cruise Routes: Jamaica is a popular port of call on Western Caribbean itineraries. These cruises depart from ports in the United States, including Miami, Fort Lauderdale, and New Orleans, and provide a convenient and entertaining way to see many places.
- ❖ Onshore Excursions: Cruise guests may visit destinations such as Dunn's River Falls in Ocho Rios, the ancient town of Falmouth, and the colorful marketplaces of Montego Bay. It is best to schedule these excursions via the cruise company to ensure a smooth and organized experience.
- ❖ Local Interaction: Cruise tourists may engage with Jamaican culture, experience Jamaican food, and enjoy reggae rhythms. Local craftsmen typically set up stalls along the ports to sell traditional Jamaican goods and souvenirs.

Private yachts and sailboats

For those looking for a more intimate and customized experience, coming to Jamaica by private yacht or sailboat is an appealing choice.

- ❖ Jamaica features well-equipped marinas, such as the Montego Bay Yacht Club and Errol Flynn Marina in Port Antonio, that cater to private yachts. Clearance processes are usually simple, with customs and immigration services accessible at major ports.
- ❖ Sailors may explore Jamaica's ports and coves while island-hopping. Each port showcases a distinct aspect of the island's attractiveness, from the verdant surroundings of Port Antonio to the vibrant energy of Ocho Rios.
- ❖ Local captains provide convenient and skilled charter services for yachts. This option enables guests to choose their itinerary, mixing rest and adventure.

Ferry services

While ferry services are not as prevalent as cruise ships or private yachts, they do give an alternate way to access Jamaica by water.

- ❖ Ferry services link Jamaica with surrounding islands, including Haiti and the Cayman Islands. Confirming

timetables and availability in advance is critical since certain services may have limited frequency.
- ❖ Ferry ports are often found in big coastal cities like Kingston and Montego Bay. These services are available to those who want to enjoy a picturesque ride and experience local maritime travel.

Recommendations

- ❖ Before sailing, review Jamaican port rules and clearance processes. Ensure that the necessary paperwork is in place to support a seamless arrival.
- ❖ Be aware of weather conditions, particularly during hurricane season. Check predictions and plan your route appropriately, with safety as the primary consideration.
- ❖ Learn about local customs by visiting marinas, fishing towns, and seaside marketplaces. Learning about Jamaica's nautical customs enriches your sailing experience.
- ❖ Practice responsible boating by following marine conservation standards. Jamaica's coral reefs and marine life are essential to the ecology. Thus, tourists are asked to reduce their environmental effects.

Finally, landing in Jamaica by boat provides a marine journey full of opportunities. Whether on a grand cruise ship, a private boat, or a beautiful ferry, travel becomes an essential part of the Jamaican experience. As you traverse the Caribbean seas, expect a warm welcome from Jamaica, where the sea and the island merge in a beautiful embrace.

How to Get Around

There are so many natural and cultural gems on Jamaica that travelers return year after year.

Whether you wish to hop from beach to beach in quest of the ideal stretch of sand or learn more about Jamaica's rich history, each part of this Caribbean gem has something fresh to offer.

So, how do you navigate your way around and discover them all? Fortunately, there are several methods to navigate the gorgeous island of Jamaica.

There are a variety of transportation alternatives available, ranging from buses and taxis to renting your vehicle. Here's all you need to know about navigating around Jamaica.

Public transportation consists of buses, route taxis, and motorcycles.

Jamaica's public transportation system comprises a network of buses and taxis connecting big and small communities around the island. The JUTC bus system serves the main cities of Kingston and Montego Bay. Coaster buses are part of Jamaica's larger bus network, often covering gaps left by JUTC buses.

There is no defined timetable or schedule for when they arrive; instead, you must embrace island time and wait for the next departure (on average, a bus or taxi will come within 15 to 20 minutes). Most large towns have dedicated bus parks or transportation hubs.

Jamaica has two kinds of taxis: charter taxis and route taxis. Route taxis operate similarly to buses and are far less expensive, with fares just slightly more than those charged by buses.

Taxi businesses operate chartered taxis, which are more costly. You phone ahead to reserve (charter) a taxi, and the firm determines the fare before your ride arrives.

Motorcycles are a common mode of public transportation in several cities, such as Negril. They operate as route taxis, transporting clients to and from certain locations across the town.

Transportation fares are best paid in cash.

The buses normally include a conductor who collects fares from each passenger. Either wait for the conductor to request all fares in cash or pay just before you leave your stop. You may pay in cash or acquire a top-up transportation card at several locations around the island.

If you take a taxi, whether a charter cab or a route taxi, you pay your fee in cash at the trip's conclusion.

Public transportation in Jamaica is reasonably safe and economical.

Remember to always board public transportation at major bus stops or terminals, be cautious at night, and carry cash in tiny denominations rather than larger amounts. Avoid using empty vehicles in route taxis. Solo female travelers may wish to avoid automobiles where males are the only occupants.

Uber is offered in various cities; however, it costs extra.

Uber does exist in Jamaica, although it is not as popular as in the United States. Drivers congregate in places like Kingston and Montego Bay. Remember that wherever there is Uber coverage, there will certainly be a (cheaper) bus or taxi choice.

Driving is the greatest method to get about in Jamaica.

While public transportation allows you to travel about Jamaica without a car, having your vehicle will make seeing the island's top spots considerably more convenient and pleasant. The roads are well-linked and easy to traverse by automobile.

All large towns have paved roads; however, they have varied degrees of potholes. Any foreign tourist should remember two important driving tenets: everyone drives on the left, and motorists (particularly taxi and bus drivers) are more aggressive on the road than you may be used to, using a "defensive" manner.

Most reliable automobile rental businesses provide unlimited mileage; nonetheless, charges in Jamaica are among the highest in the Caribbean. You may discover established local firms like Island Car Rentals and international giants like Hertz and Avis at the airport.

Private buses and drivers are available for hire.

If you don't want to drive alone, you may book a vehicle and driver for your journey (best done via your hotel). Another alternative is the Knutsford Express, a popular and reasonably priced private bus service that links major cities and tourist destinations around the island.

Even a short stroll may not be worth taking.

Jamaica is not a very walkable nation, with main cities and areas of interest widely apart. For example, the 35-minute trek from Liguanea to Half Way Tree in Kingston is difficult in the sweltering Caribbean heat, with security concerns to consider if walking at night.

Chapter 4: Accommodations

Luxury Hotels

Hyatt Ziva Rose Hall

This resort offers attentive beach and pool butlers, a Moroccan-themed rooftop bar, dazzling pools, small seaside fire pits, and Jamaica's greatest jerk chicken. Guests may experience the finest of the island's amenities, including gourmet dining, large rooms, and exhilarating land and sea activities. It's an adventure that the whole family will appreciate.

Address: Rose Hall Road, A1, Montego Bay, Jamaica.

Phone Number: 009 1 833-284-9288

Price range: from $603.

Excellent Oyster Bay.

Oceanfront beach homes, spacious living areas, and two miles of isolated, unspoiled beaches. In addition, you may enjoy a selection of foreign restaurants and bars, our world-class spa, cutting-edge fitness facility, and an unparalleled assortment of activities and services. Excellence Oyster Bay is a magnificent all-inclusive resort in a unique and picturesque environment.

Address: Oyster Bay Peninsula Coopers Pen, Falmouth JMCTY07 Jamaica.

Phone Number: 8662116223

Moon Palace Jamaica

Moon Palace Jamaica is located in the beautiful surroundings of Ocho Rios. It offers over 700 luxurious accommodations with oceanfront and partial ocean views of the Caribbean Sea, each with 24-hour room service, free WIFI, CHI-branded amenities, complimentary calls to the continental US and Canada, and more. It offers the ideal vacation for families and couples alike, with over-the-top all-inclusive amenities such as unlimited gourmet dining and snacks, top-shelf drinks, a FlowRider® Double Wave Simulator, a state-of-the-art Playroom for kids, a Teens Lounge, and world-class entertainment and nightlife. This warm-hearted resort also offers Jamaica's biggest spa, so you can indulge in some real pampering.

Address: Main Street, Ocho Rios Jamaica.

Phone: 009 1-800-943-5032.

Royalton Blue Waters, Montego Bay

Royalton Blue Waters, located in lovely Montego Bay, welcomes you to a magnificent vacation surrounded by elegant buildings, a clean beach, and a calming tropical air. This new-generation all-inclusive hotel provides discerning travelers with a family-friendly holiday experience that will attract visitors of all ages from dawn to night.

Address: Highway A1, Mountain Spring, Falmouth, Jamaica.

Phone Number: 009 1 844-631-0595

Hideaway in Royalton Blue Waters.

Rekindle your most essential ties in Montego Bay's Adults-Only (ages 18+) All-Inclusive paradise, which has swaying palm palms, a peaceful little islet, and endless sunsets over the horizon. Discover a world of gourmet restaurants, premium poolside beverages, beachfront relaxation, watersports, and nightly entertainment. Rekindle important relationships in paradise with our upgraded suite amenities, instructor-led fitness programs, and spa treatments, all within a 35-minute drive from Montego Bay International Airport.

Address: Highway A1 Mountain Spring, Falmouth, Jamaica

Phone Number: 009 1 844-631-0595

Price Range: From $526.

Hyatt Zilara Rose Hall

Hyatt Zilara Rose Hall is a sophisticated and attractive getaway for those looking to unwind from the stresses of everyday life. Couples, friends, and individuals can do anything on the resort's expansive grounds. Attentive service at every step ensures that each visitor enjoys a relaxing, stress-free holiday filled with excellent meals, beautifully crafted beverages, and memories that last a lifetime.

Address: Rose Hall Road, Montego Bay, Jamaica.

Phone Number: 009 1 833-284-9288

Price Range: From $661.

Hideaway at the Royalton Negril

Looking for somewhere to stay in Negril? Then go no farther than Hideaway at Royalton Negril, a luxurious all-inclusive resort that offers the finest of Negril right on your doorstep.

Guests may enjoy free WiFi, and rooms at Hideaway at Royalton Negril have a flat-screen TV, a minibar, and air conditioning.

During your visit, take advantage of the facilities available, such as a 24-hour front desk, a concierge, and room service. Guests staying at the hideaway at Royalton Negril may also enjoy on-site amenities such as a pool and complimentary breakfast. Free parking is offered for guests coming by vehicle.

Hideaway at Royalton Negril is conveniently near Mary, Gate of Heaven Catholic Church (3.0 mi).

While you're here, visit some seafood eateries, such as Fireman's Lobster Pit, Office of Nature, and Sun Beach, which are all close to Hideaway at Royalton Negril.

Address: Norman Manley Boulevard, A1, Negril JMDWD14 Jamaica.

Phone Number: 009 1 844-631-0595

Price range: From $844.

Sandals South Coast

Discover the unexplored. Journey to a forgotten Jamaica, where the natural beauty is remarkable. Blue mountains, luscious palm groves, clean beaches, and brilliant turquoise seas provide a stunning background for a mammoth resort on a 500-acre wildlife preserve. Sandals Whitehouse Europe Village & Spa seamlessly combines the exotic enchantment of the Caribbean with the sophisticated elegance of Europe. Fragrant greenery gardens surround charming Italian piazzas and fountains, while three European-inspired Italian, French, and Dutch towns include elegantly outfitted seaside rooms and suites. Each one has breathtaking views of the two-mile-long beach, and top-tier suites include Sandals' famed Butler Service.

Address: White House Jamaica.

Phone Number: 009 1 888-726-3257

Budget-Friendly Alternatives

Iberostar Grand Rose Hall.

Finding the perfect romantic all-inclusive resort in Rose Hall doesn't have to be tough. Welcome to the Iberostar Grand Hotel Rose Hall, a good choice for tourists like you. Guests may enjoy free internet access, and the suites at the Iberostar Grand Hotel Rose Hall have swim-up suites, a flat-screen television, air conditioning, butler service, and a stocked mini refrigerator with cold drinks. During your visit, use the services available, such as room service and a concierge. Free parking is offered for guests coming by vehicle.

Address: Main Road, Rose Hall, Montego Bay, Jamaica.

Phone Number: 009 1 877-859-5095

Coco LaPalm Seaside Resort

CocoLaPalm Resort, built in 1994, is the biggest of the tiny hotels in Negril, Jamaica. They are a family resort on Negril's 7-Mile Beach, offering non-motorized water activities, delicious dining, and thrilling entertainment for our visitors' convenience. We encourage you to come and reserve your space at CocoLaPalm, and they will keep you coming back for more.

Address: Norman Manley Boulevard, Negril, Jamaica

Price range: From $129.

Deja Resort

This 93-room All-Inclusive resort on Montego Bay's 'Hip Strip' will immerse you in Jamaica's rich culture. This unique resort is just 5 minutes from Sangster's International Airport and is surrounded by various shops, restaurants, nightclubs, and the world-famous Doctor's Cave Beach.

Address: 92 Gloucester Ave, Montego Bay, Jamaica.

Price Range: From $162.

Westender Inn

The Westender Inn, a family-owned tropical haven combining island charm with easygoing elegance, has provided the perfect Jamaican experience since 1983. The Westender Inn, a boutique hotel that embodies the island culture, is the ideal destination for relaxation and regeneration. The Westender Inn, nestled in the deep West End above the crystal blue Caribbean Sea, is your tranquil haven in paradise. Negril retreats to the Westender Inn to relax.

Address: West End Road, Negril, 03277 Jamaica

Phone: 8769574991.

Price Range: From $133.

Country Country.

Country Country Beach Cottages is the ideal of informal beach life, right on Negril's famed Seven Mile Beach. The multi-colored one- and two-story cottages have all of the anticipated conveniences (air conditioning, TV, CD-radio, verandah, hairdryer, telephone, safety box, coffee/tea, refrigerator) and are situated along a meandering route to the beach. Country Peppa Beach Grille provides a delicious breakfast daily as you enjoy the sea views. Relax and leave your concerns at home.

Address: Norman Manley Beach Boulevard, Negril, Jamaica

Price Range: From $166.

Bed & Breakfast

Great Huts

Atop a lushly wooded cliff 100 feet above the turquoise and azure waters of Boston Bay and the Caribbean Sea, there are 15 bamboo huts and a 5000-square-foot house with four big, comfortable, and elegant air-conditioned rooms. Great Huts is a one-of-a-kind village resort that honors Jamaicans' West African history while also extolling the art, wisdom, and strength of Rastafari. It is ideal for weddings and family gatherings. This tiny eco-resort has a secluded beach and two cliff-side pools with breathtaking ocean views. Over 90% of furniture, art, and décor are handcrafted by Jamaican craftsmen.

Address: 6-10 Boston Bay Road, Port Antonio, Jamaica.

Price Range: From $187.

The Blue House Boutique Bed and Breakfast Villa.

Come experience AUTHENTIC UPSCALE JAMAICA at this comfortable, casually elegant 'hidden treasure' that provides all the intimacy and charm of a small luxury boutique hotel at a reasonable price. The Barefoot Chef's highly regarded Signature No Menu Breakfasts and Three Course No Menu Dinners will highlight your visit to this FOODIE PARADISE. Before you arrive, you will be asked extensive questions about your food preferences, allergies, and limits. Once here, you'll eat excellent custom-designed meals to fit everyone's tastes.

Address: White River Estates, Ocho Rios JMCAN19 Jamaica.

Phone: 009 1 876 822-4433

Sandals Dunn's River

Rivers flow through woods on Jamaica's north coast, while thundering waterfalls dot the terrain. Love flows freely in this peaceful area, surrounded by the bounty of the Earth. Sandals Dunn's River, originally chosen by our founder for its beautiful beach and proximity to Jamaica's natural wonders, has been fully reinvented and is now part of the Sandals family.

Address: Mammee Bay Road, Ocho Rios, Jamaica.

Phone Number: 009 1 844-741-0367

Sand and Tan Beach Hotel

Sand & Tan Beach Hotel, located in Ocho Rios and a few feet from Sunset Beach, offers accommodation with a restaurant, free private parking, a beach bar, and water sports facilities. The hotel also has a private beach area and massage services. The motel has a 24-hour front desk, airport shuttles, room service, and free WiFi. The hotel will serve guests with air-conditioned rooms with a desk, a kettle, a fridge, a minibar, a safe deposit box, a flat-screen TV, a patio, and a private bathroom with a shower. Certain accommodations have a kitchenette with a microwave. Every accommodation at the Sand & Tan Beach Hotel includes bed linen and towels. This 4-star hotel offers darts, and the surrounding region is ideal for snorkeling and kayaking.

Address: White River, Ocho Rios, Jamaica.

Phone: 009 1 876 974-4613

Price Range: $110.

Polkerri's Bed and Breakfast

Polkerris and Vista de la Bahia are two homes perched on a hillside with stunning views of Montego Bay Bay. Less than a half-mile from Doctor's Cave Beach and a few minutes from the 'Hip Strip,' which has numerous stores and restaurants. The rooms are air-conditioned and have an en-suite bathroom, television, refrigerator, safe, and ironing board. A full breakfast is provided, with a variety of Jamaican and international options to select from.

Address: 13 Corniche Road, Montego Bay JMCJS Jamaica.

Seastar Inn

The Seastar Inn is only 500 yards from the majestic West End Cliffs. The accommodations are set amid gorgeous, immaculately maintained gardens. A vast array of tropical plants, trees, bushes, and flowers surrounds the property. A big, private swimming pool with a swim-up bar, pavilion, and lounge chairs is available on-site. A relaxation room with large-screen TVs, table tennis, and a pool table. The Seastar Inn also has its full-service restaurant and bar, which serves a free full breakfast and a comprehensive lunch and supper menu. Wireless Internet is available in all rooms.

Booking Tips

Planning your Jamaican vacation is more than simply picking a place; selecting the correct lodging is critical to a good trip. Here, we present an in-depth guide with helpful hints to guarantee a smooth and comfortable hotel booking procedure for your stay in Jamaica.

Define your preferences.

Consider your favorite housing style: a luxury seaside resort, a quiet boutique hotel, or a low-cost guesthouse. Jamaica has a wide variety of lodgings to suit different interests and budgets.

Place: Choose the best place depending on your interests. Do you yearn for the bustling atmosphere of Montego Bay, the cultural richness of Kingston, or the tranquil beaches of Negril? Each area of Jamaica provides a unique experience, so choose one that aligns with your trip objectives.

Conduct extensive research

Use trusted internet booking services such as Booking.com, Expedia, or Airbnb to find a variety of hotel alternatives. Read reviews from other travelers to learn about the quality of service, cleanliness, and overall client happiness.

Official Hotel Websites: Once you've narrowed your selections, visit the hotels' official websites. Direct reservations may provide special offers, extra facilities, or liberal cancellation conditions.

Consider the budget and amenities

Create a Realistic Budget:

- ❖ Determine a budget range for your accommodations.
- ❖ Remember that rates might vary based on the season, location, and amenities provided.
- ❖ Be practical about what you can spend while maintaining the overall quality of your stay.

Amenities: Prioritize amenities according to your preferences. Choose a hotel that offers the amenities you want, such as a pool, spa, beach access, or on-site dining.

Timing is important.

Peak and off-peak seasons: Jamaica's peak tourist season typically occurs in the winter. However, rates might be much cheaper during off-peak seasons. Schedule your visit around these hours to take advantage of lower prices and fewer people.

Special Offers & Packages: Watch for special promotions, discounts, and bundle packages. Many Jamaican hotels provide seasonal deals with rewards like free meals, spa treatments, and excursions.

Flexibility and Cancellation Policy

Flexibility: Choose lodgings with flexible booking rules. This is especially important during uncertain times or when your trip intentions may alter. Look for choices that enable changes or cancellations without incurring significant fines.

Understand local customs and policies.

All-Inclusive vs. Room-Only: Jamaica is well-known for its all-inclusive resorts, which provide meals, beverages, and entertainment. If this appeals to you, look into the many possibilities available. Alternatively, if you want to explore local eating alternatives, book a room-only package.

Understand the local traditions for gratuities and taxes. Some hotels automatically impose service costs, while others allow the visitor to choose. Be aware of any extra costs to prevent surprises at checkout.

Safety and Review

Inquire about the hotel's safety procedures, particularly if you are booking during a period of health concern. Ensure the hotel follows adequate hygiene and sanitation regulations to ensure your well-being.

Recent Reviews: Look for recent reviews to understand how the hotel is doing. Reviews published last few months are more likely to represent current circumstances and service quality.

Direct Communication

Contact the Hotel: Before completing your reservation, contact the hotel directly. This may be a time to clarify questions, request unique arrangements, or negotiate bespoke offers.

Package Deals

Flight and Hotel Packages: Look for bundled bargains, including flights and lodgings. Sometimes, combining these pieces might result in cost savings.

Loyalty Programs

Join Loyalty Programs: If you often visit Jamaica or intend to do so, consider joining hotel loyalty programs. Many hotels provide prizes, discounts, or special amenities to returning visitors.

Securing the ideal lodging in Jamaica involves careful consideration of your tastes, thorough research, and attention to detail. Following these detailed guidelines will help you discover the perfect location to stay and set the tone for an outstanding Jamaican experience. Whether you want to relax, go on an adventure, or immerse yourself in culture, the correct accommodations can make your stay in this tropical paradise unforgettable.

Recommended Areas to Stay

Whether planning a lifetime trip or just looking for a new vacation spot, this section, Where to Stay in Jamaica, features nine of the greatest places to stay in this magnificent Caribbean treasure.

Its sun-bleached white-sand beaches, coral reefs, swaying palm palms, and the interior's deep, lush flora and beautiful waterfalls guarantee that your days of exploration are filled to the brim.

In the nights, the seductive rhythms of Dancehall and Reggae, the vividly colored clothing of the women and the dreadlocks of the Rastafarians, dinners of Creole chicken, and a few glasses of the renowned Jamaica rum will all help you create memories that will last a lifetime.

Continue reading to learn about our top nine Jamaican vacation destinations.

Negril

Where to Stay in Jamaica for First-Time Visitors

Negril, located on Jamaica's west coast, is the perfect resort for those searching for a place to vacation in Jamaica with all the large city attractions without the noise.

Negril is commonly referred to as the resort with two sides. The beach spans five miles down the coast and is known for its spectacular sunsets. It has stunning five-star hotels and all-inclusive complexes, beach bars and restaurants, snack shacks, and souvenir stores.

The cliffs at the west end of the beach rise dramatically from the sea, housing a variety of exquisite villas, Airbnbs, mid-range hostelries, guest homes, and luxury boutique hotels. Most have amazing views of the water.

The cliff area also has wonderfully landscaped gardens where you may attend a wedding, relax with a refreshing drink while soaking up some rays, or watch the sunset.

Negril's streets are dotted with businesses, bars, restaurants, and street sellers.

On the beach, you may go snorkeling or paragliding; if you prefer something more fluid, you can join a famous alcohol cruise on a catamaran.

You can even rent your own floating bar if you're in a group. The Tiki Pon Da Sea is available for hourly rentals and has a free bar.

If you prefer action sports, JamWest Motorsports and Adventure Park is about a 30-minute from town. There, you can ride an all-terrain vehicle, race on zip lines, do rock climbing or tumble down an intense water slide into the pool below.

Kool Runnings Adventure Park is another popular destination for kids and parties, offering raft tours, water flumes, slides, go-kart racing, and paintballing.

Your nights may be as lively or quiet as you like. You may eat al fresco while viewing the sunset on Negril's clifftops or listen to reggae music at a local tavern.

If you want to party hard, go to the beach area, where there are late-night pubs, restaurants, and spontaneous performances on the beach.

Accommodation is excellent at all levels. However, seaside accommodations are likely to be more expensive.

Montego Bay

The Best Place to Stay in Jamaica for Nightlife

Landing at Sangster International Airport on the fringes of this port city allows you to be near the excitement 24 hours a day, making Montego Bay a fantastic option for your first stay in Jamaica.

Montego Bay, located on the island's north coast, is a vibrant blend of cultures that attracts tourists, residents, and expats from all over the globe.

With the bay's pristine sandy beaches, coral reefs, and warm, clear seas, you may spend your vacation hiding away in an all-inclusive resort or just relaxing on the beaches.

However, you will lose out on so much of what this intriguing island has to offer.

Gloucester Avenue, often known as the 'Hip Strip,' is located behind the seashore and is an excellent area to start adjusting to your new holiday lifestyle.

The area has several taverns, clubs, restaurants, grocery stores, souvenir shops, and reasonably priced motels.

Explore the city's history. Sam Sharpe Square is the town's focal point and the epicentre of the anti-slavery struggle in the early nineteenth century. Commanded by Sam Sharpe, who is a slave owned by an English barrister. Sharpe became a Baptist and lay deacon.

Although he was executed in 1832 for starting the anti-slavery riots, his passion set the wheels in motion, and slavery in Jamaica was abolished only two years later, on August 1, 1834.

Much of this region retains its medieval cobblestone streets and structures, including The Cage, a fugitive slave jail, and remnants of the old courthouse.

Doctor's Cave Beach, which is supposed to be supplied by medicinal mineral springs, was arguably the first to draw foreign well-heeled tourists looking to heal their numerous maladies long before the birth of the package vacation.

Other notable beaches around Gloucester Avenue include the Aqua-Sol Beach Theme Park, flumes and go-karts, and Cornwall Beach.

Rose Hall Beach and Tropical Beach are just outside the town. Most beaches have their own beach clubs, bars, and restaurants.

Away from the beach and sea, consider visiting the White Witch and Cinnamon Hill Golf Clubs and Chukka's Jungle Outpost, where you can learn about Jamaican history while zip-lining or river tubing.

If you appreciate nature and bird watching, go to Bunkers Hill Cultural Experience, where you can learn about the island's people, eat traditional Jamaican food, and feed the colorful hummingbirds.

If you prefer the ghost realm, you may discover the chilling history of the haunted Rose Hall Great House and its notorious plantation owner, Annie Palmer.

To keep the youngsters entertained, the Half Moon Equestrian Centre at the same location features ponies, donkeys, goats, and bunnies to touch.

To round off your day, you may eat, drink, and dance the night away at your all-inclusive resort or one of the numerous bars, clubs, and restaurants throughout town, particularly on the Hip Strip.

Montego Bay offers various lodging options in Jamaica, from Airbnb and guesthouses to mid-range hotels, adults-only retreats, waterfront villas, and luxurious all-inclusive resorts.

Ocho Rios

Where to Stay in Jamaica for Families

Ocho Rios is a purpose-built resort town and cruise port on Jamaica's north coast, with the island's third international airport nearby.

Ocho Rios is a popular family vacation resort featuring various activities and attractions for all ages.

A significant proportion of premium all-inclusive complexes are found here, allowing visitors to spend their vacation in pampered luxury.

Turtle Beach wraps around the bay in front of the town, dotted with luxurious hotels, all-inclusive resorts, restaurants, bars, and clubs.

If that's too crowded for you, take a 15-minute walk out of town to Mahogany Beach or take a short cab trip down the coast to Reggae Beach, the quietest of the three.

Main Street is the hub of activity in town. This bustling street has cafés, restaurants, fast food places, coffee shops, retail malls, and local markets.

Be sure to visit Island Hamlet, an open-air Jamaican-style hamlet with an amazing Reggae Museum.

Because it is adjacent to the cruise port, it is the most popular destination for cruise passengers during their time ashore. Therefore, it may be quite crowded. It is also the primary spot to visit in the evening for eating and drinking. A little reggae tossed in for good measure.

At the back, in the parish of St Anne, there are beautiful jungles, adventure parks, and the famed Dunn River Falls, making Ocho Rios an excellent base for exploring the surrounding region.

Several scheduled excursions are available, so you won't have to worry about which side of the road to drive on. Nonetheless, if you want to go your own way, automobile rental is accessible.

Did we mention the waterfalls? Dunn's River Falls flows from over 180 feet above you to the beach area below. Alternatively, you may enjoy a bird's-eye view from the overhanging bridge or the overhead zip lines that fly through the canopies.

You may visit Konoko Falls, Island Gully Falls, and Turtle River Falls nearby.

If you're looking for an adrenaline rush, try bamboo rafting on the White River or tubing through the whitewater waves down Island Gully Falls or the Blue Hole.

Whether you're a die-hard reggae lover or just like swaying to anything with a rhythm, booking the Nine Mile Tour should be at the top of your list.

Nine Mile was the birthplace of reggae legend Bob Marley, and you will hear about his journey to prominence and visit his Mausoleum.

Although the trip takes around an hour, the gorgeous road alone is well worth the time spent in your air-conditioned carriage.

If you like tropical flora and animals, visit Cranbrook Rainforest Gardens. The gardens are beautifully planned out and span over 40 acres. You may wander the grounds, view the tropical flora, and watch the peacocks.

They also feature a thrilling zip line, a charming café, and a gift store on site.

If Bob Marley is eternally associated with Jamaican mythology, so are the exploits of the Jamaican bobsleigh squad from the 1988 Olympics, which were made famous by the film Cool Runnings.

Book an adventure from Ocho Rios Pier to Mystic Mountain, where you will be hoisted high by a chair lift before flying down in your one-man bobsled. The mountain also has an infinity pool with a water shoot, a hummingbird garden, and a nature walk.

Ocho Rios has a large selection of all-inclusive accommodations and a small number of half or full-board hotels, boutique hotels, and Airbnb.

Treasure Beach

Where To Stay in Jamaica for Rustic Relaxation

If your ideal Caribbean vacation involves ancient wooden fishing boats parked on the sand, holiday shacks and cottages scattered haphazardly behind the beach, and tiny local family-run hotels, pubs, and restaurants, take a closer look at Treasure Beach.

Treasure Beach on Jamaica's southern coast comprises four little coves: Billy's Bay, Frenchman's Bay, Calabash Bay, and Great Bay.

The resort has risen in popularity from its humble origins as a single hotel over 30 years ago, yet the ecologically conscious local populace has closely managed development.

There are no huge all-inclusive complexes here. There are just a few exquisite boutique hotels, luxury villas, and wooden vacation cottages.

Surprisingly, for a resort that is so committed to maintaining its Jamaican laid-back feelings for its tourists, the Treasure Beach community, worried about boredom among the younger population, became heavily involved in sports.

A sports facility just outside the hamlet has developed exponentially since it started a few years ago. It has drawn sports stars like the

Williams sisters and Lennox Lewis, American basketball instructors, and cricket teams to train and play the young players.

Saturday evenings include a five-a-side soccer game, a tongue-in-cheek talent show, and DJ performances. A popular evening among both residents and tourists.

There is also a local Natural History Museum about a mile outside town. The four little bays are all quite similar. Few beaches feature beach shacks for food and beverages, so check ahead.

You may wear a beach towel, but be careful while swimming since the water might get rough with an onshore wind.

Evenings are often quiet, with few food options. There are a few great seafood restaurants and others that provide foreign cuisine, such as pizza.

Don't expect to drink all night, either. However, landlords have been known to work longer hours if the Red Stripe or Jamaican rum is flowing and the till jingles.

Accommodation is limited compared to larger resorts, so if rustic and laid-back is what you're looking for in Jamaica, book early.

Kingston

The capital and cultural hub of Jamaica.

Kingston, located on Jamaica's southeast coast, became the country's capital in 1872 and is now the island's enormous economic and cultural core.

Visitors may reach the town core less than 30 minutes from Jamaica's second international airport, located just south of the city in the bay's outer harbor.

Although there are nine magnificent Caribbean beaches along Kingston's waterfront, they all seem delightfully uncommercialized, with Kingstonians using them mostly on days or weekends off.

Others are white sand, black sand, and others are a combination of sand and stones. There are no high-rises or all-inclusive condominiums here, just the occasional restaurant, tavern, or snack shack.

Choose your Favorite place to relax after a day of touring. Regardless of the beach you select, there will be plenty of room to put your blanket down and relax.

However, the situation in town is rather different. Despite catering mostly to business travelers rather than visitors, hotels and apartment complexes abound, with the most popular neighbourhood being uptown, New Kingston, where you are never far from the excitement.

During your stay in Kingston, you may visit the following attractions:

- ❖ The National Gallery of Jamaica is located on Ocean Boulevard.
- ❖ The Bob Marley Museum is located at 56 Hope Road.
- ❖ Devon House, approximately 1881, located at 26 Hope Road.
- ❖ Life Yard on Fleet Street.
- ❖ Liberty Hall Museum, 76 King Street.
- ❖ William Grant Park, aka 'Parade'
- ❖ Tuff Gong Recording Studios, 220 Marcus Garvey Drive.
- ❖ Alpha Boys School Arts Centre at 26 South Camp Road.
- ❖ Coronation Market.

Various stores, pubs, cafés, and diners are located throughout the port area, the world's seventh-largest natural harbor. With so much to do in the city and so much of Jamaica's culture to discover, it's no surprise that few tourists visit the beaches.

You'll discover many local and foreign eateries to dine at in the evenings. In addition, there are pubs, clubs, and entertainment places to accommodate every musical taste.

One word of caution: like any major city, Kingston has its fair share of pickpockets, scam artists, and muggers. Be a bit streetwise. Stick to well-lit streets at night, remain with the crowd, and never walk off alone.

Accommodation is numerous in all places, although, as previously said, it is targeted more toward foreign business travelers than vacationers.

Runaway Bay

Where to stay in Jamaica for snorkeling and scuba diving.

Runaway Bay, located in Saint Ann Parish on the island's north coast, between Montego Bay on the west and Ocho Rios on the east, has all you need for a full, off-the-grid, peaceful, laid-back vacation in Jamaica.

One of the main attractions of Runaway Bay is that it is seldom overcrowded with cruise ship visitors.

Most of the hotel accommodations are all-inclusive and positioned along the gorgeous beachfront, with several establishments claiming exclusive beach sections for their guests.

There are open-fronted beach bars, food shacks, and souvenir huts along the beaches.

Runaway Bay has just one main street lined with all-inclusive, full-board, and half-board hotels, but there are also some villa and boutique hotel accommodations and a few stores, bars, and restaurants around the town.

Travel to Cardiff Hall Beach or Fisherman's Beach if you aren't staying by the water. Both offer dazzling sandy beaches and crystal clear shallow water for a long way out.

With its offshore coral reefs and many colorful reef fish, the region is popular with snorkelers and scuba divers.

If you want to get away from the beaches, the town offers an 18-hole golf course, and there are tours available to destinations like Nine Mile Village, the home of reggae artist Bob Marley, the Green Grotto Caves just outside the village, and the majestic Dunn's River Falls.

If you want a bit more, the bustling resort of Ocho Rios is within around a 30-minute drive.

Dining-out menus are often limited in diversity, with a focus on indigenous Jamaican cuisine. However, various seafood restaurants deliver the freshest fresh seafood, as well as others offer outstanding curries.

There is plenty of international and local alcohol available in the bars, but what better way to finish the ideal vacation in Jamaica than to lounge at a beach bar watching the sunset while drinking a colorful Caribbean cocktail?

Port Antonio

A laid-back resort ideal for surfers and outdoor sports.

Port Antonio has had a mixed history, beginning as one of Jamaica's early tourist attractions and sinking into an area of crime and squalor before rising again to become one of the island's most laid-back visiting locations.

Port Antonio is located on Jamaica's northeastern coast and is about a two-hour drive from either Kingston or Ocho Rios, depending on which airport you arrive at.

It was formerly a major port for banana and coconut exports, but it is now the island's third-biggest port, with a purpose-built marina where some of the largest boats in the Caribbean are often seen docked in the bays.

It is one of Jamaica's most photographed sites, with the Blue Mountains in the background and slopes of deep green tropical flora flowing down to the water's edge, soft white sand beaches, and blue sea. It has also been used as a setting in several important films.

The beaches are, as usual, nice and not too commercialized. Frenchman's Cove has a curved lagoon where freshwater meets the ocean. Boston Beach (where Boston jerk chicken was developed) draws a few surfers due to its higher-than-average waves.

While visiting Winnifred Beach, you will see artist Rastafarians selling their sculptures and local fishermen repairing their nets.

Port Antonio also has a strong interest in the music industry, with some recording executives establishing studios in some larger hotels.

Songwriters and producers gather to shape new works and create content for some of the most popular vocalists in the UK and US. It's no surprise, therefore, that most pubs in town make music a large part of their appeal.

Port Antonio town is far less frantic than the larger resorts of Montego Bay, Ocho Rios, and Negril, and it attracts more people from the United Kingdom and Europe than the States.

Nonetheless, you should be able to locate all you need in the area's stores and marketplaces.

Similarly, while the options are limited, eating out at a local restaurant or having a beverage at a local bar is a terrific way to unwind after a long day touring the interior.

Port Antonio has a decent variety of self-catering flats, private rentals, villas, and a few mid-range hotels.

Mandeville

Where to Stay in Jamaica for Ecotourism.

Mandeville may be particularly appealing to visitors who like ecotourism and learning about their chosen area's culture, architecture, ecology, and animals rather than beaches.

Mandeville, located 2,000 feet above sea level on the Manchester plateau in Jamaica's west-central highlands, is a bustling but relaxing mountain town surrounded by lush greenery and near many of the island's natural attractions.

Founded in 1816, it was primarily a working town with a sizable expat population, many former British military officers. It became a significant boom town in the 1950s when bauxite mining began in the vicinity, and it has never looked back since.

Today, it serves as a marketplace for local farmers and producers. It is home to the bulk of personnel from two mining firms, and there is a growing ex-pat population of elderly Jamaicans who have returned home after years working overseas.

It is also becoming a popular location for those searching for somewhere to stay in Jamaica to get up close and personal with the island's people, nature, animals, and tropical vegetation.

Don't think that since Mandeville lies in the island's center, it must be a one-horse town; it is far from that. Tropical flowers may be everywhere throughout town, including gardens, pots, tubs, and window baskets.

Old colonial residences from the nineteenth century may be seen all around the center. Enjoy a stroll around Mandeville Square with fountains, sculptures, and a war monument.

The Mandeville Courthouse, erected in 1817, is located across from the park, and St. Mark's Anglican Church, completed in 1816, is nearby.

Several scheduled tours are available where you can participate in a wide variety of activities. Look into visits to Apple Valley Park, Marshall's Pen, and Black River Safaris.

There are also public-access private gardens, as well as horticultural groups and exhibits.

Manchester Country Club, founded in 1865, has an 18-hole golf course. Alternatively, you may sample spirits at the Appleton Estate Rum Experience or get your coffee fix at the High Mountain Coffee Factory.

There are many retail malls across town to meet your every need, the largest of which is Manchester retail Centre.

There are several cafés, coffee shops, pubs, and high-quality restaurants to satisfy every taste, as well as theaters, discos, and nightclubs to keep your nights interesting.

Falmouth

A Historic town with a contemporary cruise terminal.

Falmouth, in the parish of Trelawny, is a historic port town on Jamaica's north coast just 18 miles from Montego Bay.

Founded in 1769, the port, the town, grew in prominence until the early 1800s when the sugar and rum trades peaked.

Falmouth's fortunes dropped after the Abolition of Slavery Act of 1834, although it continued to trade as a port town and build new houses.

This time, with many of its original Georgian-style buildings still surviving, gave the town its distinct, historical character and gained it both United Nations World Heritage and Jamaican National Heritage designations.

Falmouth's fortunes have changed again. With the inauguration of the brand-new cruise ship facilities in 2011, prosperity has returned to the town, and an increasing number of non-cruise visitors are booking accommodations in the region.

Although several beautiful Caribbean beaches in the vicinity require some driving, two of the nearest are Time & Place Beach and Burwood Beach.

Although it is enjoyable to explore at your leisure, organized excursions are highly suggested to get the most out of this historic location, and there are several options.

A guided Walking Heritage Tour is an excellent opportunity to learn about the area's history while strolling through streets set out in the 1700s, with most of the original buildings still surviving.

Visit the historic courthouse, completed in 1815, and return to the era of plantations and slave trade.

If you're becoming hooked on Jamaican food, try taking an arranged Culinary Tour, where you'll get to sample the finest Jamaica has to offer.

Other trips include visiting the Glistening Waters Luminous Lagoon, normally open at night and allowing you to soak in waters teeming with (harmless) bacteria that glow in the dark.

A Trolley Tour, in which a trolley bus-like vehicle transports you about town. If you want to be more active, try paintballing, river rafting, or tubing.

If you wish to eat away from your hotel some nights, travel to the port area, which has a variety of local and foreign restaurants and pubs.

Ask your hotel for suggestions if you wish to dine and drink in town. When visiting a new nation, it's usually a good idea to be street-smart.

There is a wide selection of housing options, including homes and flats, Airbnb, mid-range boutique hotels, premium villas, and 5-star hotels.

Chapter 5: Exploring the Beauty of Jamaica.

Top attractions

There are several compelling reasons to visit Jamaica, including the music, food, and beaches. But did you know this Caribbean country also has some of the world's most breathtaking waterfalls, caves, and swimming holes? In reality, there are almost 4,200 square miles of magnificent mountains and rainforests to discover.

Because it would be impossible to explore Jamaica's natural attractions* in a single trip, we compiled a list of our favorites—and noted which areas they are located in—to help you plan your next holiday.

Dunn's River Falls

Location: About three kilometers from Ocho Rios in St. Ann Parish.

Dunn's River Falls may not be as impressive as Niagara or as tall as Olo'upena, but it is still worth a visit. This breathtaking waterfall, nestled behind a canopy of lush green trees, is the ideal spot to seek relief from the scorching heat. The 160-foot-high tower comprises a succession of terraces, and visitors are invited to climb it to swim and rest in the natural pools.

The attraction is so lovely that you could think it was man-made, yet every corner, hole, and crack was created by the river running straight into the Caribbean Sea.

Blue Hole Mineral Spring

Location: About 10 kilometers from Negril in Westmoreland Parish.

If you've embraced the health travel trend, take notice of this natural attraction in Jamaica: blue holes, vast sea caves made of limestone, are supposed to have therapeutic effects.

To experience the advantages of this mineral spring, you must leap from a 24-foot-high cliff (or walk down a ladder if you prefer). While swimming in the pool is enough to relax, you can also have an exfoliating massage for an extra fee at a neighboring facility.

Martha Brae River

Location: Trelawny Parish is located around 19 miles from Montego Bay.

There are two sorts of people in the world: those who seek out adrenaline-pumping sports such as whitewater rafting and those who take advantage of any chance to float down a tranquil river.

If you fall into the latter category, make sure Martha Brae is on your list of must-see natural sites in Jamaica; it provides one of the greatest river-rafting experiences on the island. As you enjoy the scenery from your bamboo raft, a professional guide will tell you about the flora and animals and the tale of Martha Brae, a local witch who safeguarded buried wealth from settlers.

Barney's Flower and Hummingbird Garden

Location: About 5 kilometres from Negril in Westmoreland Parish.

Did you know Jamaica is home to five different species of hummingbirds? Black-Billed Streamertails, Red-Billed Streamertails, Vervain Hummingbirds, Ruby-Throated Hummingbirds, and Jamaica Mango Hummingbirds are all found on this Caribbean island, and many may be seen in their native environment at Barney's Flower & Hummingbird Garden in Negril.

When you visit this quarter-acre property, you will be given a private tour of a tropical garden and an up-close look at some of the birds, flowers, and plants that make Jamaica so vibrant and beautiful.

Green Grotto Caves

Location: About 20 kilometres from Ocho Rios in St. Ann Parish.

Sometimes, the world's beauty is best seen underground. The Green Grotto Caves provide limitless corridors as you approach an underground lake. Swimming is not permitted, but the stunning stalagmites and stalactites that cover the cave's floor and ceiling more than compensate.

Take a deep breath if the mere thought of this natural draw causes you to experience claustrophobia. The caverns are fairly big, so you won't have to crawl or wriggle through narrow spaces to enjoy the view.

Negril Cliffs

Location: About 4 kilometres from Negril in Westmoreland Parish.

This is one of Jamaica's most popular cliff jumping spots—and not only because of the stunning bluff that rises 40 feet above sea level. Rick's Café, positioned at the summit, also attracts a large audience.

Established in 1974 (when Negril was still a small fishing community), the restaurant and bar draws visitors who like diving, swimming, partying, and watching the sunset. If you want to see a natural site without leaving the city, here is the place to go.

YS Falls

Location: About 34 kilometres from Montego Bay in St. Elizabeth Parish.

The primary distinction between YS Falls and Dunn's River Falls is their position; the former is on the island's southwest side, while the latter is on the northeast side. This implies that you will most likely visit one or both depending on where you are staying in Jamaica.

Aside from that, the two natural attractions are pretty similar. YS Falls is also made up of multiple terraces (there are seven in total), giving it a perfect place to swim and relax in nature. Remember to wear your water shoes! They will make it simpler to ascend the stairs near the falls and reach the rope swings dangling over several pools.

Luminous Lagoon

Location: Trelawny Parish is located around 23 miles from Montego Bay.

A visit to Luminous Lagoon, which is well-called for its bioluminescent waters, is the ideal way to spend an evening in Jamaica. Boat cruises in the region run around 45 minutes, giving you ample time to see the vivid blue light. You may also swim in the lagoon, surrounded by the dinoflagellates (plankton) that provide the sparkling effect**.

You'd be remiss not to include this natural occurrence on your schedule since it happens in just a few places throughout the globe.

Blue and John Crow Mountains

Location: About 50 km from Ocho Rios in Portland Parish

Hiking lovers will enjoy visiting Jamaica's sole national park, which spans 100,000 acres of tropical, highland rainforest. Established in 1993, it is home to many of the island's distinctive flora and animals, including the Giant Swallowtail butterfly, which you can see when hiking to the peak.

We suggest beginning your trek early to avoid the heat and capture a beautiful dawn. If you're not a morning person, don't worry; you may visit a Blue Mountain coffee farm before leaving; these local farms produce some of the world's greatest beans.

Reach Falls.

Location: Portland Parish is located around 86 kilometres from Ocho Rios.

What distinguishes this waterfall from the others on this list? Reach Falls is a single rock face surrounded by a tiny river pool, unlike Dunn's River Falls and YS Falls, which feature many falling water levels. At first look, this seems to be a great location for sunbathing, but there is much more to discover.

The surrounding region is an outdoor playground with secret caverns and small swimming holes to explore. Daredevils are welcome to leap down the Rabbit Hole, while more fearful tourists may seek safety in the heart-shaped holes known as "natural Jacuzzis."

Historical Landmarks

Jamaica's magnificent sights will never depress you. Jamaica's stunning highlands, jungles, beautiful coastal resorts, and coral-lined beaches beg you to explore.

The gorgeous Caribbean Island nation offers an unforgettable holiday. If you're planning a trip to Jamaica and aren't sure what to see, this list is for you! Jamaica has a rich history that has resulted in historic and modern sites.

When Christopher Columbus (1451-1506) came to Jamaica in 1494, it had already been colonized by the Arawak and Carib aborigines. The Spanish colonizers conquered Jamaica in 1655 and rapidly enslaved its indigenous people.

Slavery was abolished in 1838, and since they no longer owned land, liberated Africans became indentured workers on plantations. The island won independence from Britain in 1962, joining the Commonwealth of Nations.

Allow my firsthand knowledge to take you through what to anticipate and see when seeing this beautiful nation. Plan your unforgettable trip to Jamaica today and explore the list of stunning sights in Jamaica!

Fort Charles

Address: One Queen Street, Port Royal, Jamaica

If you like history, you might consider visiting Fort Charles. It is located in Port Royal, a tiny port town established at the entrance to a natural harbor. The English erected Fort Charles, the first fort in Port Royal town, to secure the area they had won from the Spanish.

Fort Cromwell was named after Oliver Cromwell, the Parliamentarian Lord Protector of England. In 1662, the fort was renamed Fort Charles.

It was built to resemble a battleship, with guns around the external walls to deter intruders. This did not deter the Native Americans, who, with the help of their French allies, sacked the fort in 1689.

The fort lost its importance in 1692 when a terrible storm devastated it. It has, nevertheless, maintained most of its look and has become an important part of Jamaican cultural heritage.

Its principal attractions include the Museum, the Giddy House, and the Battery. The Giddy House was built in 1888 to store firearms and ammunition. The term Giddy residence refers to the sentiments that visitors get when they visit the residence. This is owing to the 45° tilt caused by the earthquake in 1907.

Emancipation Park

Address: Oxford Road and Knutsford Boulevard, Kingston, Jamaica

The saying says, "Emancipate oneself from mental slavery. "Nobody but ourselves can free our minds" at the park's entry perfectly summarizes the park's tale. This park is themed "Tribute to Freedom."

The entryway has a huge sculpture of a man and woman staring up at the sky, symbolizing the abolition of the slave trade; the majority of Jamaicans are derived from Africans who were forcefully taken to the Caribbean and Americas as slaves.

The Liguanea Club donated this 7-acre plot of land to the Jamaican government as a gift for constructing Emancipation Park.

When you arrive at Norman Manley International Airport, the park is about a half-hour drive away. The Jamaica Pegasus Hotel is across the street from the garden and offers great accommodations.

The large number of immigrants formed a new parish (St. Andrew/Uptown), to which the wealthy merchants migrated. The 1907 earthquake drove even more residents from Downtown Kingston to Uptown.

Emancipation Park offers a variety of activities, including a jogging route, a little gym, and gorgeous flowerbeds. Take a walk in the park and enjoy the calm atmosphere and pleasant breezes.

Emancipation Park was built in 2002 and inaugurated on July 31, 2002, the day before Emancipation Day, which is commemorated on August 1.

Bob Marley Museum

Address: 6, 56 Hope Road, Kingston, Jamaica.

The hometown of reggae legend Bob Marley has a rich history of providing for his admirers and the rest of the globe. Mrs. Rita Marley, Bob Marley's widow, renovated the iconic musician's former house into a museum six years after his death. It is one of Jamaica's most renowned sights.

Bob Marley's Museum is around a ten-minute drive from Emancipation Park. The journey from Kingston Railway Station to the Museum will take around 30 minutes. You may also take a bus to drop you off near the museum.

The unsuccessful murder attempt on Bob Marley took place on December 3, 1976. His residence was searched a few days before he was scheduled to play at the Smile Jamaica Peace Concert. Bob was shot in the arm, but he survived and continued to work for peace in third-world nations.

Museum tourist attractions include an 80-seat theater, a gift shop, and a picture gallery. Various tours are available, including the Bob Marley Home Tour, Bob Marley's "Making of the Music Tour," and the Combo "One Love" Tour.

After your museum tour, you may relax and enjoy excellent meals at the One Love Café. This is one of the most popular attractions in Jamaica.

Seville Great House

Address: CQPM+7RC, Priory, Jamaica.

There is a rumour that the soul of Annie Palmer, the violent female plantation owner, haunts the Seville Great House. She was dubbed the white witch who haunted the Rose Hall grounds in Montego Bay.

The Seville Great House was built to symbolize English triumph after the Spaniards abandoned it in the mid-17th century. It was established in 1745 by the grandson of a British Army officer, Captian Hemmings, governor of New Seville.

Originally, the home had two levels, but it was reduced to one by 1898. No one renovated it until 2010 when the rebuilding of the Seville Great House and Heritage Park began.

The Great House provides daily guided tours and an artifact collection. The museum also hosts an informative display of property dating back to A.D. 650. This includes DVDs that display simulations of what things looked like in the past.

Good Hope Estate House

Address: C89F+24J Wakefield, Jamaica

This historic Jamaican monument was erected on an estate owned by John Tharp, one of Jamaica's greatest landowners. Though constructed in England in the contemporary Georgian style, the Good Hope Estate House was modified to better fit Jamaican climate. Hip roofs were installed to help it resist Caribbean storms.

When it comes to entertaining vacation activities, you have plenty of options both on and off the resort. The Good Hope Estate House's beach is about 25 minutes away.

The mix of the sea, sand, and mountains provides the whole Jamaican experience in one spot. Activities include zip line, dune buggy excursions, and river kayaking. You may also lease an ATV to visit the full 2000-acre property.

If you're traveling with family, friends, or business colleagues, you may stay in one of the Good Hope Estate House villas. The admission cost is variable for those who wish to view the site without participating in any additional activities.

Mayfield Falls

Address: 3254 Norman Manley Boulevard, Negril, Jamaica.

The Mayfield Falls, located along the Mayfield River, comprise 21 cascades. The highest (9.8ft) is known as the "Washing Machine" and is big enough to accommodate most persons behind the falls.

Mayfield Falls is situated in a picturesque setting, complete with lush vegetation and local Jamaican animals. You will most likely witness many native bird and butterfly species.

The mountain walk offers beautiful views, and it takes about 1-2 hours to get to the waterfall. It would be ideal if you hired a tour guide to cover all of the falls on your trip. A skilled guide will almost certainly have suggestions for enhancing your trip experience.

Mayfield Falls may be a terrific vacation for families, couples, or lone travellers. The river does not have strong currents; even when it rains, they are moderate, making it quite safe for children. There are several tours available depending on your budget. There are additional activities like horseback riding.

Devon House

Address: 26 Hope Road, Kingston, Jamaica.

Devon House has a long history; it was erected in 1881 in the late Georgian rather than the current Victorian style. The owner was George Stiebel, the son of a Jamaican housekeeper and a German Jew.

George Stiebel became Uptown's first black Jamaican millionaire (St. Andrew). He acquired his riches in Venezuela before returning home to become the Custos (civic custodian) of St. Andrew.

Devon House has undergone two restorations since it was designated a National Monument on January 23, 1968: the first in 1968-9 and the second in 1974. The second refurbishment was done in the Victorian style.

Devon House is open for tours, and you've returned to 1881 Jamaica. Take a tour of the estate, including the well-kept and elegantly furnished dining room and a glimpse inside the master bedroom.

The house tour takes around 30 minutes. Tours are provided Monday through Friday, 9 a.m. to 4 p.m. The mansion is closed on Christmas Day and Good Friday. When hungry, head to the Devon House courtyard and choose from the several pubs and eateries.

Chapter 6: Exploring Jamaican Beaches.

Best beaches in Jamaica

Jamaica's nicest beaches are famed for their pristine white sand and crystal blue seas. Despite its tiny size, Jamaica has some of the world's most stunning beaches, rivaling Italy, Thailand, and Australia. You can go from beach to beach in minutes by automobile.

Jamaica's remote beaches provide a complete escape. Others are even more vibrant, offering fresh seafood, water sports, and live music. If you like beach vacations, Jamaica's various beaches provide an ideal balance of excitement and leisure. Continue reading to learn about these must-see Jamaican shore beauties.

7 Mile Beach

An infinite Negril beach with a blue ocean.

Negril's Seven Mile Beach is Jamaica's longest, making it simple to get away from it all while being close to luxurious services. Located on the bustling Norman Manley Boulevard, you'll never be far from an air-conditioned restaurant or your hotel.

One of Jamaica's greatest beaches, the enormous expanse of white sand is greeted by shallow turquoise seas that are quiet enough for families to enjoy snorkeling and paddleboarding. Several pubs, beach loungers, and restaurants are nearby; everything is conveniently located.

Open: daily from 10 a.m. to 10 p.m.

Fort Clarence Beach

Picnics on the beach and family-oriented activities

Fort Clarence Beach is between Jamaica's Great Salt Pond and Hellshire Bay, so you'll feel surrounded by brilliant blue sea on all sides. This is a popular neighbourhood spot for picnics with reasonable beach furniture rentals. It also features beach volleyball courts for sports enthusiasts.

Fort Clarence Beach is ideal for families since it is less congested than other beaches in Jamaica and has lifeguards on duty. When you've had enough fun in the sun, local restaurants and beach bars provide shelter and refreshment.

Open: daily from 9 a.m. to 5 p.m.

Hellshire Beach

A bustling beach with great seafood, chilled beverages, and reggae music.

Hellshire Beach has a dynamic environment with a lot going on, making it ideal to combine a beach and a party. Locate a location for your towel and then explore the many food sellers and bars dotted throughout the beach.

This beach is always packed with music and dancing, which continues until late. You may also have a seaside massage and sample some famed Jamaican food. The fried fish at Hellshire Beach is reputed to be among the finest in the nation.

Open: 24/7

Doctor's Cave Beach

A beach club for individuals who want a catered experience.

Doctor's Cave Beach is where you want security, convenience, and exceptional service. Doctor's Cave Bathing Club operates this private beach, and they will care for your every need while you rest on a comfortable beach bed or enjoy a meal or drink while watching the sea.

There is no shortage of activities here. You may do scuba diving, snorkeling, sailing, kayaking, etc. A trip on a glass-bottomed boat provides stunning views of marine life without getting your feet wet. Lifeguards are also on duty, so this beach is safe for families.

Open: daily from 8:30 a.m. to 5:30 p.m.

Phone: +1 876-952-2566.

Turtle Beach

A bay to relax in peace.

Turtle Beach in Ocho Rios Bay is conveniently accessible for a swim, yet it is less crowded than other prominent Jamaican beaches. There aren't as many pubs, restaurants, or activities here, which is a positive for people who want a more relaxing atmosphere.

You don't have to bring a picnic if you want to eat or drink at Turtle Beach. There are merchants along the strip and watersports and boat tour operators, albeit not as numerous as elsewhere. Turtle Beach is one of the quietest beaches without venturing far off the usual road.

Open: daily from 8.30 a.m. to 4 p.m.

Phone: +1 876-656-8031.

Long Bay Beach

A quiet bay away from the tourist crowds

Long Bay Beach is one of Jamaica's most remote beaches. It's also incredibly long, so you can easily locate your little beachfront part with no one else around. Strong currents and larger waves make this a popular surfing area, but new swimmers should be cautious.

The beach is nearly abandoned, so you won't find many conveniences here. There are a few food sellers and little guesthouses, but that's about it. It's a Favorite hangout for hikers and artists who arrive for a day and remain for weeks. Our second word of caution: you may never want to leave.

Open: 24/7

Lime Cay Beach

Like having an own island all to yourself.

Lime Cay Beach is situated on Lime Cay Island, approximately 2 miles off the coast of Kingston. It can scarcely be termed an island since the little patch of a beach is just 100 meters long and not nearly as broad. But great things come in little packages, and the scenery and snorkeling here are unparalleled.

people on Lime Cay take their boats out for picnics on weekends. Go throughout the week to avoid crowds and feel like you're on your little Caribbean Island. Remember to bring some food and beverages with you since there won't be much else on the beach save sand and sun.

Open: 24/7

Water Activities

With its crystal-clear Caribbean seas and diverse marine life, Jamaica is an aquatic playground for those seeking exhilarating water sports and undersea activities. From peaceful bays to exciting surf, here's a comprehensive introduction to Jamaica's broad range of water activities.

Scuba diving

Reef Exploration: Jamaica has an abundance of magnificent coral reefs filled with marine life. Dive aficionados may visit areas like Montego Bay Marine Park, Pedro Bank, and Ocho Rios' underwater caverns. With different depths and habitats, these locations appeal to divers of all skill levels.

Wrecks & Underwater Landmarks: Discover sunken gems and historical shipwrecks dotted throughout Jamaica's coast. Notable locations include the wreck of the MV Xtabi in Negril and the Katherine shipwreck in Port Royal, which provide a unique combination of history and aquatic life.

Snorkeling

Coral Gardens and Lagoons: Snorkeling in Jamaica allows you to explore vivid coral gardens and lagoons for a more relaxing aquatic excursion. Doctor's Cave Beach in Montego Bay, Discovery Bay's sheltered waters, and Runaway Bay's shallow reefs are popular snorkeling destinations.

Guided excursions: Join guided snorkeling excursions conducted by professional instructors who will show you the greatest sites and provide insights into the local marine life. Many resorts and tour companies provide equipment rentals and guided excursions to ensure your snorkeling experience is pleasurable and safe.

Windsurfing

Thrills on the Waves: The winds around Jamaica's coastline provide great conditions for windsurfing, drawing both novice and experienced surfers. Negril's Seven Mile Beach and the seas around Ocho Rios are especially popular windsurfing destinations, combining calm waters and spectacular waves.

Instruction and Rentals: If you're new to windsurfing, many water sports establishments provide instruction and equipment rental.

Expert instructors can walk you through the fundamentals, assuring you a safe and pleasurable time on the waves.

Kitesurfing

Adrenaline-Pumping Action: Jamaica's consistent trade winds make it an ideal location for kitesurfing. The coastlines of Hellshire Beach and Long Bay in Portland are famed for their constant winds, making them perfect for kitesurfing lovers looking for an adrenaline thrill.

Training and Safety: Before hitting the waves, consider training from a licensed kitesurfing school. Safety is crucial, and instructors can teach you basic skills, kite control, and water safety to ensure a fun but safe experience.

5. Jet skiing:

Zoom Across the Caribbean: Feel the exhilaration of the Caribbean air as you glide across the blue waves on a jet ski. Jet ski rentals are available in popular beach spots such as Negril, Montego Bay, and Ocho Rios, allowing you to explore the coastline while experiencing the thrill of this high-speed water activity.

Age and license Requirements: Be aware of the age and license requirements for jet skiing in Jamaica. Operators usually conduct a short orientation to ensure passengers understand safety requirements and navigation restrictions.

Kayaking

Explore Coastal Wonders: Take a kayak trip across Jamaica's tranquil coastal locations. Explore the mangroves, secluded coves, and peaceful lagoons. Kayak lovers may enjoy gorgeous courses along the Great River in Montego Bay and the Rio Grande in Portland.

Guided Tours & Sunset Paddles: Take a guided kayak trip to improve your experience and learn about the local environment. Sunset paddles along the coast are a lovely and relaxing way to conclude your day on the ocean.

Deep Sea Fishing

Cast Your Line in Caribbean Waters: Jamaica has outstanding deep-sea fishing options for those looking for a new kind of aquatic activity. Charter boats are offered in major fishing destinations such as Montego Bay and Ocho Rios, where you may try your luck with marlin, tuna, and mahi-mahi.

Many fishing tours in Jamaica have skilled crews that know the finest areas and tactics. Whether you're an experienced fisherman or a beginner, the team can guide and support you during your fishing trip.

Parasailing

Fly Above the Coastline: Parasailing provides an exciting way to fly above Jamaica's coastline. You may enjoy panoramic views of the beaches and blue oceans from the spectacular heights. Parasailing is popular at Seven Mile Beach in Negril and Doctor's Cave Beach in Montego Bay.

Safety Briefings: Before taking off, operators usually conduct a safety briefing to guarantee a safe and happy parasailing experience. Follow their instructions for an unforgettable journey in the skies.

9. Stand-up paddleboarding (SUP):

Balance on the Waves: Stand-up paddleboarding (SUP) is becoming more popular in Jamaica, providing a unique opportunity to explore the calm seas around the coast. For a relaxing and gorgeous experience, try SUP in Frenchman's Cove in Portland or the Blue Lagoon in Port Antonio.

Rentals and instruction: Many water sports establishments provide SUP rentals and instruction for beginners. Before you begin your SUP trip, learn the art of board balance and paddling methods from qualified instructors.

Safety Advice for Water Sports in Jamaica:

- Wear necessary safety equipment, such as life jackets and helmets.
- When participating in sports such as scuba diving, windsurfing, and kitesurfing, follow trained instructors' supervision.
- Stay in authorized swimming and water sports zones for your safety.
- Check weather conditions and follow recommendations while participating in water activities.
- Protect yourself from the sun by staying hydrated and using sunscreen, particularly in tropical areas.

Jamaica's waters provide a wide range of water activities, offering to both adrenaline seekers and those looking for a more relaxing aquatic experience. Whether diving into the depths, surfing the waves, or exploring the shore, Jamaica's colorful marine environment welcomes you to go on an aquatic adventure.

Chapter 7: Savouring Jamaica: Culinary Experiences

Must-Try Dishes in Jamaica

Jamaican cuisine is distinctive, with meals and beverages inspired by immigration from diverse parts of the globe, including India, Africa, and China. Jamaican cuisine packs a culinary punch unlike any other, thanks to the variety of spices, herbs, and tastes in practically every dish, including scotch bonnet peppers, allspice, and coconuts. So, to ensure you don't miss out on JA's wonderful cuisines, snacks, and beverages, we've compiled a list of must-try items. Consider it a TO DO LIST, and feel free to check items off as you do them!!

Typical Jamaican dishes

Ackee and Saltfish

Ackee and Saltfish are Jamaica's national meals, eaten mostly for breakfast. It is often served with boiling green bananas, breadfruit, Johnny cakes, and boiled dumplings. Yeah, I know, all of that is for breakfast! Ackee, Jamaica's national fruit, is a brilliant red tropical fruit with whitish flesh that may be cooked. Did you know that if Ackee is eaten before it is ripe, it produces a deadly gas that kills anybody or everything that consumes it within 24 hours? Crazy stuff, but don't worry, you'll be alright if you eat Ackee in Jamaica since Jamaicans know what they're doing. Plus, we're still here, and it's one of our favorite Jamaican foods.

Curry Goat

This is an Indian-influenced meal; if you've never tried goat before, this is definitely one of the finest ways to introduce it. Curry goat was formerly a meal reserved for rare occasions, but it can now be enjoyed anytime. This dish is often served with rice, peas, and a carrot-cabbage salad.

Oxtail

Yes, this is precisely what you expect, but it tastes far better. At one time, this section of the ox was considered scrap meat, and only impoverished households ate it. However, as the affluent discovered how wonderful oxtail was after Big Mother gave it some gentle love and care, it became a costly delicacy all over the globe. However, Jamaican oxtail is unlike any other.

Escovitch Fish

The fish (King Fish, Snapper) is frequently marinated overnight to increase its taste before being fried the following day. It is served with a spicy vinegar dressing prepared from onions, carrots, peppers, and scotch bonnet pepper. Escovitch fish is eaten yearly but is particularly popular on Good Friday and Easter.

Callaloo

A leafy green with a texture similar to spinach, although I believe it is more like collard greens. Cod or saltfish is often used as the major ingredient. Callaloo may also be a side dish with onions, tomatoes, garlic, and carrots.

Ital Dish

In Jamaica, you must eat an Italian meal prepared by a real Rastafarian. Ital means vital, indicating that the ingredients utilized are pure and natural, with no preservatives, processed additives, or other weird things in our food these days. Just pure nourishment, like nature intended. I defy you to consume anything that has not been processed, bleached, or genetically engineered!

Typical Jamaican Sides

Festival

This was by far my favorite side dish at JA. Festival is a fried dumpling made with cornmeal, flour, salt, and sugar, contributing to its distinct flavor! This side is frequently served with jerked pork or fried fish.

Bammy

Another fave of mine! Bammy is a flat, circular bread prepared from grated cassava (yucca) that may be cooked, steamed, or baked. I like the baked ones since the fried ones are too oily for my taste. This site may be served with any dinner, making an excellent to-go snack.

Fried dumplings.

Fried dumplings, often called Johnny cakes, are similar to festivals but less sweet. Johnny Cakes are fried dumplings made from flour often eaten for breakfast.

Bread Fruit

This fruit, an excellent starchy replacement for bread, goes well with various cuisines and may be steamed, boiled, baked, fried, or roasted.

Popular Restaurants to Eat

These fantastic Jamaican eateries include fresh seafood, grilled meat, and various vegan and vegetarian options. This island may be your gourmet heaven if you like flavorful, spicy foods influenced by cultures worldwide. Pair your dinner with a Jamaican beer or handmade drink to better understand the local culture.

So, where can you get the greatest native and Caribbean-inspired foods in Jamaica? Whether you prefer a restaurant that serves seafood harvested that day, a rooftop deck in the city, or a thatched house in the hills, Jamaica offers it all.

Devon House

Enjoy breakfast at a historical estate.

Devon House is a fashionable brunch place that combines Georgian and Caribbean architecture. Its trademark puff pastry pie works nicely with local sweets, including bread pudding, sweet potato pudding, and rum cake.

Devon House features a spacious outside lawn that is ideal for picnics. Treat yourself to Devon House ice cream, which comes in flavors like Devon Stout and rum raisin. The bakery is open till 10 p.m. every day. It's busiest around midday most days, so go late in the afternoon to escape the crowd.

Location: 26 Hope Road, Kingston, Jamaica

Open: daily from 10 a.m. to 10 p.m.

Phone: +1 876-926-0815.

Miss T's Kitchen

Traditional Jamaican food served in a tropical atmosphere

Miss T's Kitchen is a cozy Jamaican restaurant along the shore in the port town of Ocho Rios. You may sample genuine meals, including curried goat, grilled lobster, and honey-fried chicken. There are also lots of flavourful vegetarian and vegan options.

Miss T's Kitchen is a popular destination with residents in the early afternoons and during lunchtime; however, lines are usually short. Try one of the restaurant's freshly squeezed juices for a refreshing treat after a day of visiting the island.

Location: 65 Main Street, Ocho Rios, Jamaica.

Open: daily from 12 to 11 p.m.

Phone: +1 876-795-0099.

Scotchies

A local destination for Jamaican jerk chicken.

Scotchies is a prominent Jamaican restaurant known for its genuine Jamaican jerk chicken. Other delicacies known as festivals include roasted breadfruit and fried sweet dumplings. The meat-smoking procedure is said to be more than 500 years old.

Scotchies has three locations, with the most popular being near Montego Bay. It's normally busiest around dinnertime on Fridays, but you can get a table anytime without waiting too long.

Location: Montego Bay, Jamaica.

Open: daily from 11 a.m. to 11 p.m.

Phone: +1 876-953-8041.

M10 Bar and Grill

Fresh Jamaican seafood meals and a large beverage menu.

M10 Bar & Grill began as a truck stop but has now evolved to become one of the island's most popular destinations for fresh Jamaican seafood. Choose a lobster thermidor or a surf and turf if you want to go all out. Other popular menu items include red pea soup, oxtail stew, and cow foot with beans.

M10 Bar & Grill is located in the Jamaican capital, Kingston, near the Jamaica Defence Force Air Wing. Monday is often the slowest day for the eatery. If you want a busier setting, go there for supper on Fridays.

Location: 6 Vineyard Road, Kingston, Jamaica.

Open: Monday, 11 a.m. to 5 p.m.; Tuesday and Wednesday 11 a.m. to 11 p.m.; Thursday through Saturday 11 a.m. to midnight; and Sunday

Phone number: +1 876-930-2112.

Lorna's Catering

A top-rated restaurant serving Jamaican basics

Lorna's Catering is a takeaway restaurant in Kingston that serves dishes such as curry goat, brown stew, fish fillets, and oxtail and beans. Side dishes include cornmeal dumplings, macaroni salad, and stir-fried pak choi. Pair your meal with freshly squeezed June plum natural juice for health benefits.

Lorna's Catering is noted for its prompt service and genuine Jamaican cuisine. It's only open from 11 a.m. to 3 p.m., making it a popular spot for a late breakfast or lunch with locals.

Location: 189 Mountain View Avenue, Kingston, Jamaica

Open: Monday through Saturday from 11 a.m. to 3 p.m. (closed on Sundays).

Phone: +1 876-978-5865.

EITS Cafe

Jamaican and European-inspired cuisine with woodland vistas.

EITS Café offers farm-to-table cuisine with views of the Blue Mountains. The menu combines European and Jamaican cuisine, with most ingredients from the restaurant's organic garden. Popular dishes include savory crepes, mountain mango chutney, and barrel-roasted chicken. For something unique, try one of the restaurant's customizable salads.

EITS Café's location gives a respite from the heat and activity of Kingston. It's around 45 minutes distant from the city center.

Location: 17 Mile Post in Newcastle, Jamaica.

Open: daily from 9 a.m. to 6 p.m.

Phone: +1 876-367-8191.

Little Ochie's Seafood Restaurant and Bar

Traditional fish meals are cooked to request.

Little Ochie Seafood Restaurant & Bar is a thatched-roof beach hut in the peaceful community of Alligator Pond. You can see local fishermen carry their daily catch straight to the restaurant, making it an excellent opportunity to eat cooked-to-order, fresh Jamaican seafood.

Its position on Jamaica's southern coast makes it an ideal site to interact with the people and learn about Jamaican culture. If you want to make your seafood meal, there's a fish and lobster market just around the street from Little Ochie Seafood Restaurant & Bar.

Location: Alligator Pond Post Office, Alligator Pond District, Jamaica.

Open: daily from 8:30 a.m. until midnight.

Phone: +1 876-852-6430.

Summerhouse

A refined gastropub offering cuisine ideal for sharing.

Summerhouse offers a blend of Jamaican and Caribbean food. This restaurant, located in a 19th-century structure, is excellent for a romantic night out with your significant other. Citrus-infused fish meals, local sausages, and various grilled alternatives make it popular among the locals. The East Indian meze plate is ideal for sharing.

m Book beforehand if you want a table for lunch or supper on the weekend. If you want to escape the crowds, visit Summerhouse during the week when reservations are typically not required.

Location: Harmony Hall in Ocho Rios, Jamaica.

Open: Wednesday through Friday from 11 a.m. to 7:30 p.m., Saturday from 10 a.m. to 7:30 p.m., and Sunday from

Phone: +1 876-858-0031.

Chapter 8: Shopping in Jamaica

The greatest locations to shop in Jamaica

The greatest shopping in Jamaica is divided between bustling marketplaces and tranquil shopping centres. You won't find the newest high-end brands here, but Jamaica is known for its trendy beachwear and one-of-a-kind handcrafted products.

Several of the greatest shopping experiences are available in and around Montego Bay, but you'll be well served anywhere you travel in Jamaica, particularly for beachwear and gifts. When visiting markets, take the necessary steps to be discreet with valuables and always keep your items with you.

Main Street, Jamaica

High-end retail complex in Montego Bay

Main Street Jamaica (previously The Shoppes at Rose Hall) is one of Jamaica's greatest luxury shopping destinations. There is an emphasis on locally manufactured, high-quality things such as jewelry, homeware, and clothing. A wonderful assortment of souvenirs, particularly quality ingredients, are also available to replenish your kitchen cabinets back home. Several eateries and booths ensure that you will not go hungry.

The open-air mall is on Jamaica's north coast in St Bran's Burg. It is attached to the Montego Bay Convention Centre and bordered by some of the island's most luxurious 5-star resorts.

Location: Main Street, Rose Hall, Jamaica

Open: Wednesday through Friday from 9 a.m. to 5 p.m., Saturday from 9 a.m. to 4 p.m. (closed Sunday and Tuesday.

Phone: +1 876-953-3245.

Coronation Market

Soak in Kingston life in this bustling hive of activities.

Coronation Market is a bustling market filled with attractive vendors offering a wide range of unique food. The large, iron-covered market, affectionately known as "the stomach of Jamaica," is noted for its assortment of farmers' market booths, which sell delectable fruits and vegetables, fresh meats and seafood, spices, and cooked meals.

Coronation Market sells more than just wonderful cuisine; it also attracts charismatic sellers from all over the island who offer textiles, vehicle parts, electronics, music, apparel, and ofanything

else. The lively market is an excellent place to ab
while looking for discounts and a one-of-a-kind ch
unfiltered Jamaican life only a few feet away from th
circuit.

Location: Pechon Street, Kingston, Jamaica

Open: Monday through Saturday from 5 a.m. to 10 p.m. (closed on Sundays).

Island Village, Jamaica

Duty-free shopping in Ocho Rios

Island Village Jamaica is a tourist-centred retail complex in front of the Ocho Rios cruise port. It welcomes waves of visitors to its beautiful grounds, which have stores and booths arranged like a town around a central lawn.

The products for sale here are mostly Jamaican souvenirs, such as jewellery, clothing, cigars, and liquor. Most things are duty-free, resulting in significant savings for international tourists. Because everything is open air, the ideal time to explore Island Village Jamaica is in the morning or late afternoon. Try to avoid Wednesdays since they are particularly congested for cruise passenger arrivals.

Location: Turtle River Road, Ocho Rios, Jamaica

Open: daily from 8 a.m. to 10 p.m.

Phone: +1 876-613-3719.

Kingston Craft Market

Search for unique products in Jamaica's capital.

Kingston Artisan Market has a huge range of waterfront vendors offering an almost limitless variety of Jamaican artisan products. The market on the seaside in downtown Kingston provides stunning ocean views while shopping for souvenirs and trinkets.

The Kingston Craft Market's friendly stall owners offer locally made and Jamaican-themed items, apparel, artwork, and memorabilia to provide a welcoming shopping location for visitors. You'll also discover plenty of tasty food and drink to keep you going while you look for the ideal presents to take home. Feel-good reggae music reverberates throughout this bustling market, making it a very pleasurable place to spend a few carefree and sun-soaked hours.

Location: 174 Harbour Street, Kingston, Jamaica.

Open: Monday through Saturday from 7 a.m. to 6 p.m. (closed on Sundays).

Musgrave Market

Shop for fresh vegetables in Port Antonio.

Musgrave Market is a local shopping destination in Port Antonio, Jamaica's northeast coast. This farmers' market features the island's finest natural goods, including fruit and vegetables, local crafts and wonderful street cuisine. Because this is aimed toward locals, you can be sure you're getting the real Jamaica, unlike the more tourist-oriented markets in Montego Bay. Most purchases are often less expensive.

Musgrave Market is easily accessible from Port Antonio's central seaside route. The market is open six days a week, although it is best visited on Saturday mornings.

Location: West Street, Port Antonio, Jamaica.

Open: Monday through Saturday from 9 a.m. to 1 p.m. (closed on Sundays).

Pavilion Mall

Kingston offers hassle-free shopping.

Pavilion Mall is a secure and easy area to shop in Kingston, with many things available. Although the costs are higher than downtown, this is a convenient shopping option for families and couples.

You'll find clothing, books, gadgets, hairdressers, and the usual shopping complex amenities. There are other banks here as well. If you feel hungry, there are a variety of restaurants providing regional cuisine and a food court with inexpensive and lively local specialties.

Location: 2-4 Constant Spring Road, Kingston, Jamaica.

Open: Every day from 8 a.m. to 7.30 p.m., and on Sundays until 9.30

Phone: +1 876-926-1236.

City Centre Shopping Mall

A huge, contemporary mall next to Harmony Beach in Montego Bay.

City Centre Retail Mall is a huge, contemporary retail mall in the heart of Montego Bay. It's a recognizable landmark with a diverse range of stores within. You may find something for the whole family here, from clothes to jewellery to gadgets.

You'll discover many American products here, a smart choice if you need anything special while visiting Jamaica. Prices are established and will be comparable to what you would pay in other countries for identical goods. Food-wise, you'll be primarily confined to franchise fast-food restaurants, which are at least quick and handy.

Location: Fort Street, Montego Bay, Jamaica

Open: daily from 9.30 a.m. until 10 p.m.

Phone: +1 876-993-2616.

Best souvenirs to buy

Jamaica is well-known for various attractions, including breathtaking waterfalls, beautiful beaches, and thrilling excursions. Jamaica is also one of the top Caribbean islands for souvenir buying, which we'll cover in this part.

To discover the ideal Jamaican memento, consider what stood out during your vacation. Another important consideration is who you want to give the present to and what they like. You may need to browse around to discover the greatest deals. Popular gifts on this island include locally crafted t-shirts, paintings, Blue Mountain Coffee, and spicy sauce. To assist you in deciding on the finest selections, we have produced a list of the 18 greatest Jamaica souvenirs. They would make an excellent gift to take home after your stay!

Reggae music and memorabilia.

Reggae started in Jamaica. This is the best island to visit if you want to immerse yourself in reggae music and perhaps discover new songs while on vacation. There are numerous reggae musicians on this island, and you may discover others you've never heard of while you're there. In addition to reggae, there is a wide variety of local music to enjoy. Popular genres on this island include dancehall, dub, and ska. Many of the local taverns and clubs will be playing these tracks. During your Jamaica holiday, you'll be able to buy albums you won't find anywhere else; they make ideal gifts or keepsakes.

If you want to learn more about reggae, consider visiting the Rasta community at Mount Debre Zeit in Papine, Kingston. Mount Debre Zeit Records and Variety Store are excellent souvenir possibilities. While immersing yourself in the island's reggae tunes, drink one of the locally prepared root tonics and talk to the locals about the island's music and performers. Bob Marley, Jimmy Cliff, Greggory Isaacs, Shaggy, and Sean Paul are among Jamaica's most well-known musicians.

Expert tip: The Bob Marley Museum is an excellent tour stop for reggae lovers, particularly Bob Marley devotees. This site has a gift store where you may purchase souvenirs and a wealth of information on the artist's life and inspiration.

Blue Mountain Coffee

Blue Mountain Coffee does not require much introduction; it is one of the world's most well-known coffee brands. Blue Mountain Coffee's exclusivity contributes to its popularity, as does the fact that the coffee beans are hand-picked and cultivated at high altitudes, which impacts their quality. Blue Mountain Coffee is popular because of its low bitterness and rich taste.

Blue Mountain Coffee is cultivated on volcanic soil in Jamaica's Blue Mountain area. This coffee may be expensive because of the complexity involved in its manufacturing process. Despite this, it is still highly sought after and considered one of the greatest coffees in the world. While in Jamaica, you may purchase Blue Mountain Coffee as a present. See the Coffee Industry Board of Jamaica accreditation logo to ensure your Blue Mountain Coffee is real.

Oil paintings and other artworks

If you want to bring some unique artwork home, buy an original oil painting in Jamaica. There are many possibilities available, all made by brilliant local artists. Some variants include sunsets, blue seas, beautiful beaches, village life, and festivals. This is an excellent way to bring part of the beauty of Jamaica home with you.

You may explore some local galleries to discover the right oil painting or other piece of artwork. This is also an excellent method to be inspired to commission your artwork. Depending on the size, it may be possible to have your artwork sent straight to your house. You may be allowed to take it as a carry-on if it is tiny enough.

Jamaican Rum (and Rum Cream)

Jamaica has many rum distilleries that create high-quality brands. So, why not take home some of Jamaica's greatest rum as a souvenir? Several types of rum are available, including white rum, golden rum, aged rum, and overproof. Wray & Nephew White Overproof Rum, Worthy Park Estate Rum-Bar White Overproof Rum, Hampden Estate Pure Single Rum 46% ABV, and Appleton Estate 12-Year-Old Rare Blend are excellent choices.

The wonderful thing about local rum is that it always adds the right touch to every drink. Try some of Jamaica's rum creams if you like something more mellow. Some kinds provide nuts, spices, and even dried fruits. Rum Cream pairs wonderfully with Blue Mountain Coffee, so they may make the perfect Jamaica memento. Keep in mind that Jamaica's legal drinking age is 18. Anyone under that age will not be legally permitted to buy alcohol on this island.

Hot sauce.

Many Jamaican recipes, particularly jerked meats, are known for their strong spice levels. Even if you don't order from a prominent jerk restaurant, you may add some heat to your meal with a bottle of spicy sauce. Scotch bonnet peppers, among the hottest chili peppers in the world, are often used in Jamaican hot sauce. If you buy this as a souvenir, you'll be able to present a gift full of fire, flavor, and, of course, a touch of Jamaica. When it comes to Jamaican spicy sauce, you have several alternatives. Milder variations are also available, including fruits like mango and banana.

Coconut oil

Some people believe that coconut oil may be used to treat almost everything. When visiting Jamaica, don't miss the opportunity to get local cold-pressed coconut oil. This oil may be used for various purposes, including hair and skin care, makeup removal, and several health benefits. According to health experts, coconut oil is one of the healthiest oils available; it is said to help protect the body and brain. Because of its many health advantages, this will make an excellent present; be sure to get some for yourself too!

Jerk seasoning

If you fall in love with jerk chicken, jerk pig, or even jerk shrimp while visiting Jamaica, the good news is that you may take some jerk spice home with you and try to reproduce these dishes on your own. Jamaican jerk spice is a fantastic keepsake, but remember to get some for yourself. Walkers Wood and Island Spice are the greatest jerk seasoning brands, which may be obtained in local supermarkets and gift stores.

Jamaican beef patties.

Beef patties are one of the lovely things Jamaica is renowned for. While on vacation, you may have fresh and tasty beef patties at some renowned restaurants. Because these patties are so delectable, you may wonder whether you can take some home with you. Well, good news! You can! We acknowledge that it may need some forethought, but if all goes well, you can carry frozen patties home to share with friends and family. Once you are home, you only have to heat them and dive in. Freeze them and pack plenty for sharing, plus a few for yourself.

Cookbooks

Jamaica's cuisine contributes to its uniqueness. Purchasing a local cookbook is an excellent way to bring some incredible cuisine home. This might make an excellent keepsake, especially for someone who has never been to Jamaica. You may also use the cookbook's recipes to prepare an authentic Jamaican supper for your friends and family. This will be an excellent way to share your experiences in Jamaica with those you care about.

Chapter 9: Nightlife in Jamaica

Overview of nightlife scenes.

Jamaica, a bustling Caribbean island famous for its rich culture, reggae music, and breathtaking scenery, also has a thriving and diversified nightlife scene. From seaside parties to reggae clubs and local taverns, Jamaica has a wide range of entertainment choices once the sun goes down. This complete introduction will look at prominent locations, music genres, cultural influences, and safety concerns in Jamaican nightlife.

Reggae music and dancehall: the heartbeat of Jamaican nightlife.

Jamaica's nightlife is known for its world-renowned reggae and dancehall music. Visitors may immerse themselves in captivating rhythms and deep songs at various music venues.

Kingston, the capital, is a popular destination for reggae fans, including notable places such as the Bob Marley Museum and dancehall establishments like Famous Nightclub.

Beach Parties and Resorts: Tropical Vibes Under The Stars

- ❖ Jamaica's beautiful beaches change into lively party hotspots at night. Beach parties are often held at coastal resorts, integrating local and international music, fire performances, and wonderful Jamaican food.

- ❖ Negril's Seven Mile Beach and Montego Bay's Hip Strip provide a variety of beachside bars and clubs to suit all preferences.

Local Bars and Rum Culture: An Authentic Jamaican Experience

- ❖ Exploring neighbourhood bars offers a real experience of Jamaican nightlife, which is heavily influenced by local culture. Visitors may relax, engage with locals, and experience Jamaica's varied rum culture.
- ❖ Pelican Pub, a rustic offshore pub, provides a unique location for sipping cocktails, meeting locals, and admiring beautiful views of the Caribbean Sea.

Festivals and Special Events to Celebrate Jamaican Culture.

Jamaica offers diverse festivals and special events that celebrate music, art, and culture. The Reggae Sumfest in Montego Bay and the Bob Marley Birthday Celebration in February are must-see events for music fans.

Safety Concerns: Enjoying Nightlife Responsibly

- ❖ While Jamaica is typically safe for travelers, it's important to be cautious and follow local norms. Stick to well-known and recognized establishments, travel in groups, and avoid dimly lit or unknown regions.

❖ While engaging with locals might improve your experience, remaining aware of your surroundings and possessions is important.

An unforgettable nightlife experience in Jamaica.

❖ Jamaica's nightlife scene combines music, culture, and tropical feelings. Whether dancing to reggae sounds in Kingston, drinking rum on a beach in Negril, or visiting local pubs, Jamaica's after-hours scene is guaranteed to create an impact.

Jamaica's nightlife is a vibrant mix of music, culture, and tropical atmosphere. From the throbbing sounds of reggae and dancehall to the relaxed ambiance of beach parties and local pubs, the island offers many possibilities for unique and unforgettable nightlife experiences. As with any location, adopting responsible travel assures a safe and pleasurable journey through Jamaica's thriving after-dark scene.

Popular nightclubs and clubs.

Pulse 8 Nightclub

Location: Trafalgar Road in Kingston.

Pulse8 is a popular nightclub in Kingston with a vibrant ambiance and broad music selection. The club routinely holds themed parties and events with prominent local and worldwide DJs.

Opening hours: Thursday through Saturday: 10:00 PM - 4:00 AM.

Fiction Fantasy Nightclub

Location: 2-4 Phoenix Avenue, Kingston.

Fiction Fantasy Nightclub is a fashionable venue in Kingston that plays a mix of reggae, dancehall, and worldwide music. The club's beautiful design and cutting-edge sound system add to its appeal.

Opening hours: Wednesday-Sunday: 9:00 PM-3:00 AM.

Quad nightclub

Location: 20-22 Trinidad Terrace, New Kingston.

The Quad is a lively nightclub with a broad music selection, including reggae, dancehall, hip-hop, and electronic dance music.

The facility has various floors and VIP areas, offering a dynamic nightlife experience.

Opening hours: Friday and Saturday: 11:00 PM to 4:00 AM.

Tracks and Records

Location: Marketplace, 67 Constant Spring Road, Kingston.

Tracks & Records, founded by Jamaican sprinter Usain Bolt, is a unique sports bar and nightclub. Guests may enjoy a relaxed ambiance, tasty cuisine, and a diverse drink menu while listening to various music genres.

Opening hours: Monday-Sunday: 11:30 AM-2:00 AM.

Margaritaville Ocho Rios.

Location: Island Village, Ocho Rios.

Margaritaville is a prominent franchise with outlets around the Caribbean. The Ocho Rios branch is well-known for its beachside location, vibrant atmosphere, and themed events. The club often showcases live concerts and DJ sets.

Opening hours: Monday-Sunday: 10:00 AM-2:00 AM.

BlueBeat Ultra Lounge

Location: Rose Hall, Montego Bay.

The Blue Beat Ultra Lounge in Montego Bay has an upmarket and refined setting. The club combines live music, including jazz and reggae, to create a comfortable but elegant atmosphere.

Opening hours: Thursday-Saturday: 8:00 PM-2:00 AM.

These nightclubs are only a sampling of Jamaica's vibrant nightlife culture. Before arranging your night out, check with the individual venues to see if their opening hours have changed or if there are any special events. Enjoy Jamaica's vibrant and varied nightlife!

Live Music Venues: The Best Places to Experience Reggae

Jamaica's greatest locations to hear reggae are largely concentrated around Kingston, the island's capital city. After all, it's the epicenter of Jamaican musical culture, with hundreds of pubs and clubs playing excellent dub, rocksteady, reggae, and ska till late. The city also has great museums dedicated to the careers of music luminaries such as Bob Marley and Peter Tosh.

Reggae can be found around the island, so it's worth investigating outside Kingston. Jamaica's countryside, sandy beaches, and rural communities all have some connection to the Rastafari movement. Plan your vacation around a major reggae festival (typically held in February or July) to see performances by well-known performers from across the globe.

Kingston Dub Club

Enjoy high-quality music from Jamaica's top sound system.

Kingston Dub Club is a bustling Jamaican nightclub that plays high-quality ska, rocksteady, and reggae. It is famous for housing Rocker's Soundsystem, one of the greatest on the island. The club's vividly painted speaker stacks pump out bass-heavy roots reggae and dub music every Sunday.

Due to its dynamic environment, the club is crowded with passionate dancers and reggae fans till late. You may enjoy delicious cocktails and Italian cuisine (a vegetarian diet popular in Jamaica's Rastafari movement). Kingston Dub Club is located in the hills of St. Andrew and offers stunning views of the metropolitan skyline.

Location: 7b Skyline Dr., Kingston, Jamaica

Open: Sunday, 8 p.m. to 2 a.m.

Phone: +18768151184.

Reggae Sumfest

A weeklong celebration in Montego Bay.

Reggae Sumfest is one of Jamaica's major music events. It takes place in mid-July and includes several festivities at various sites in Montego Bay. The event has included performances by Beyoncé, Jay-Z, Ludacris, Alicia Keys, Usher, Lil Wayne, Rihanna, and Mary J. Blige.

Reggae Sumfest typically begins with a beach party on Tropical Bliss (Sunday) and a street dance event at Old Hospital Park (Monday). Other events include theme parties, conferences, and workshops. The main event is a two-day festival with some of the world's top dancehall and reggae performers.

Nine Mile

A site of pilgrimage for Bob Marley admirers.

Fans of Bob Marley's reggae music will like Nine Mile. The town in the Saint Ann countryside serves as Marley's birthplace and ultimate resting place. The Bob Marley Mausoleum, housed in a modest church near his boyhood home, is a must-see attraction. This modest facility has a large collection of Marley's guitars, trophies, and photos.

Nine Mile is about 142 kilometres northwest of Kingston. Tours departing from Jamaica's capital are available for visitors wishing to spend a few hours at Marley's birthplace.

Redbones' Blues Café

Enjoy performances by prominent reggae artists in Jamaica.

Redbones Blues Cafe is a long-running family-owned Kingston restaurant featuring live music. Since 1976, it has been a popular spot to hear reggae in Jamaica. Its stage has hosted notable musicians from genres, art exhibits, international films, and poetry readings.

Redbones Blues Cafe is busiest on Fridays and Saturdays when jazz and blues acts go on until late. The restaurant specializes in Caribbean and fusion foods, ideal for a pleasant supper (and performance) in Kingston.

Location: 2 Renfrew Road, Kingston, Jamaica.

Phone number: +1 876-978-6091.

Dubwise Jamaica

Since 2013, this has become a worldwide sound system event.

DJ Yaadcore established Dubwise Jamaica, a famous sound system event, in 2013. The annual session is normally held on Barbican Road, near the Orchid Village Plaza. You can anticipate a high-energy environment owing to the excellent dub reggae performed by notable local and worldwide performers. You could even see Yaadcore at the turntables, joined by reputable artists.

Dubwise Jamaica began as a weekly night dub session in Kingston and has now spread to numerous cities across the globe, including Miami, Brooklyn, and Trinidad.

Festival and Events

Events to Add to Your Calendar

Bob Marley Celebrations

When? February.

February is a great month to visit Jamaica for more than just the warm weather. Every year, a week of festivities commemorates the greatest reggae music star. The Bob Marley Museum hosts several events, including karaoke competitions, fashion displays, exhibits, and concerts.

International Reggae Day

When? July.

This day-long celebration honors the impact of reggae music on Jamaican culture and throughout the globe. The event focuses on bringing people together via music, media, and communication, with many tributes to Bob Marley, the original king of reggae.

Jamaican Food and Drink Festival

When? October.

If you and your group like eating, add Jamaica's Food and Drink Festival to your itinerary. Spend five days on the island, experiencing the best dishes and greatest stars in Jamaica's culinary sector. Try local Favorites like jerk chicken and crispy pig belly before delving into foreign treats like Peking duck and sushi.

Harbour Fest

When? December.

Does spending your next New Year's Eve on an island paradise seem appealing? Join hundreds of people to witness free fireworks as you ring in the New Year on Kingston's Down Town Harbour.

Chapter 10: Itineraries

10 days in Jamaica.

Day One: Exploring Negril's Shoreline.

Drive down to Negril from Montego Bay and relax on Seven Mile Beach. This stretch of beach is the final sandy area before reaching Negril's iconic stony cliffs. If you're searching for an alcoholic beverage and live reggae at night, I suggest Alfred's Ocean Palace, Drifter's Bar, and Bourbon Beach.

Day Two: Cliff Jumping at Rick's Cafe.

-Wake up and have breakfast at Sweet Spice. Our buddy, who lives in Jamaica, suggested this home-style eatery. Do you need more convincing?

-How can you visit Negril without leaping 35 feet into the crystal-clear blue ocean at Rick's Cafe? After breakfast and beach time, travel to Rick's for late lunch/early supper before plunging down the notorious cliffs. This restaurant is recognized for having the greatest view of the sunset in Negril, so stay and enjoy a cold one as the sun falls into the water.

Day 3: Swimming at Blue Hole Mineral Spring.

-Leave for Treasure Beach in the morning, but first, stop at Blue Hole Mineral Springs. This seldom-visited hole in the ground is filled with deep blue spring water and is the ideal location to unwind and escape the scorching Jamaican heat. For $10, you may enter the park, relax by the pool, indulge at the bar, or leap 24 feet into the hole. Arrive early if you want the place to yourself. We came when they initially opened and were virtually alone for about two hours.

-Stop at Cloggy's On The Beach for a quick lunch before continuing to Treasure Beach. This roadside restaurant and tavern offers seaside seating and tasty food.

-After you've arrived at your temporary abode, relax at Jake's Restaurant, an oceanfront sanctuary.

Day 4: Relaxing at Treasure Beach and Floyd's Pelican Bar.

-Awaken and hire a boat to Floyd's Pelican Bar, a tiki bungalow half a mile offshore. A boat excursion from Treasure Beach will take around 25 minutes and cost about $ 5,000 JAD per person. The price per person decreases as the number of people in your party increases. Your Captain is unlikely to want to remain out there all day, so make it clear that you are more than willing to stay if he receives another tour. He assured us we wouldn't want to be out there for more than an hour, so we were thrilled when, 45 minutes later, he got another tour and raced back to pick them up. We spent three hours at Floyd's and never regretted being "stranded."

-After a long day of drinking in the sun (and red stripe), go to the beach and unwind at Jack Sprats Bar and Restaurant. Don't forget to get some ice cream on your way out. I particularly suggest the stout taste, produced using the island's Dragon Stout.

Day 5: Explore Port Antonio

-In the morning, get up and travel to Port Antonio. It is a lengthy ride, so an early start is recommended. The roads you travel to get there make it a long journey, not the distance itself.

-Stop at Lover's Leap before continuing on your journey. According to legend, two enslaved lovers jumped to their deaths from the 1700' cliff when their lord fell in love with the lady and intended to sell her lover to another estate, permanently separating them. While the narrative is quite gruesome, the view from the restaurant is stunning.

-When you get to Port Antonio, stop at Blue Lagoon. This secret bay boasts some of the deepest blue water you've ever seen and is worth visiting. Pro Tip: You are free to visit Blue Lagoon on your own, and there is a parking lot at the bottom of the hill if you simply want to check it out. Don't be pressured by the locals at the park entrance to take a boat ride. There are numerous vendors, and you can catch a ride at the bottom of the hill. There is no entry cost.

Day 6: chasing waterfalls.

-Now that you're on Jamaica's eastern coast wake up and watch the sunrise from the breathtaking cliffs of Great Hut's Eco-Resort. The views from these cliffs are breathtaking, and you will most likely be able to enjoy them alone. Most people dislike getting up early on vacation, but with so much to do, there isn't much time for sleep.

-Get in the car and drive to Reach Falls. This is another attraction where locals offer private tours as you drive into the area. Again, don't feel pressured to book with them if you want to see the "government side" of the falls, as we did. If you drive into the park, you will pay $10 per person and can swim in the falls themselves. The private tours can only walk you up to the falls, but you will inevitably not be allowed into the park's space. Finally, I recommend visiting the falls through the Urban Development Corporation. Operating hours are Wednesday through Sunday, 8:30-4:30. Pro Tip: Be sure to ask a lifeguard/tour guide to take you to the "rabbit hole." You'll take a short walk upstream, where your guide will show you to a cavity among the rocks to jump into a hidden swimming cove. Note: a tip is expected, and the experience is worth it!!!

-Go relax on your private beach and plunge off the cliff into Lynches Bay. Ensure you are a strong swimmer; the current can be challenging sometimes.

-Have dinner at Boston Jerk Centre for some authentic Jamaican cuisine. The locals will be clamouring to get your business, so feel free to haggle a little; you can eat a delicious meal that won't break the bank.

Day 7: Resort Relaxation

-We treated ourselves to an all-inclusive on our last full day, considering we had a 6-hour drive from Port Antonio to Montego Bay. It was a great way to close out our week of adventure and relax and recharge before heading back to reality.

-Spend some time at Doctor's Cave Beach. This beach offers beach chairs and umbrellas to rent, a restaurant with sea-side service, and water trampolines so you can relax or play the day away however you'd like. Using these facilities is charged a fee, but your hotel or resort may cover it, so check at the front desk before heading over.

-Hit the Hip Strip at night for some bar hopping, and don't forget to score some grub from a jerk chicken cart to celebrate the ending of your vacation in paradise.

Day 8: Homeward Bound

-If time permits, lounge on the beach one last time.

-Return your car and head for the airport.

Chapter 11: Practical Advice and Tips for Visitors

Local Etiquette

Jamaica is known for its lively culture, friendly people, and laid-back lifestyle. Navigating local customs is critical for tourists seeking a courteous and pleasurable encounter. Here is a comprehensive guide to local manners in Jamaica:

Greetings and Communication

- ❖ Jamaicans are noted for being friendly. Always smile and say "Hello" or "Good morning/afternoon/evening."
- ❖ When addressing someone formally, use respectful titles like "Mr." or "Mrs." followed by their last name.

Respect for the Elders

- ❖ Respecting elders is firmly rooted in Jamaican society. When talking with the elderly, use respectful words and gestures.
- ❖ Offering Seats: When using public transit or in busy areas, giving your seat to older folks is normal.

Table manners

- ❖ Washing hands before meals is standard practice. This approach is seen as respectful and sanitary.
- ❖ Jamaican meals are often shared communally. When invited to someone's house, be willing to share food and explore local delicacies.

Clothing and appearance

- ❖ Jamaicans value modesty in attire. When attending public venues or holy locations, dress modestly.
- ❖ Beachwear: Covering up is recommended outside of resorts and beaches.

Punctuality

Jamaican time may be more flexible compared to other cultures. While punctuality is encouraged, do not be shocked if activities begin later than expected.

Religion and spirituality

- ❖ When visiting churches or other religious locations, dress modestly and respectfully. Always get permission before snapping photographs.
- ❖ Jamaicans embrace spirituality in their everyday lives. Be open to religious talks, but avoid difficult themes.

Socialization and Invitations

- ❖ Accepting invitations to someone's house is considered nice. Bringing a little gift, such as local chocolates or flowers, is a kind gesture.
- ❖ Jamaicans value personal space despite their amicable nature. Avoid standing too near during a chat.

Tipping

Tipping is a common practice in Jamaica's service industry. In restaurants, a 10-15% tip is appreciated. Also, tip hotel workers and tour guides for excellent service.

Language

Patois: Although English is the official language, many Jamaicans speak Patois (a local dialect). Attempting a few Patois terms might be seen as a gesture of appreciation for culture.

Safety and security

Awareness: Follow local safety standards and use caution in new regions. Keep valuables protected and be attentive to your surroundings.

Visitors to Jamaica who follow these local etiquette conventions may make good contacts, appreciate the rich culture, and contribute to a harmonic cultural exchange.

Safety and Health Tips

General Safety Guidelines

Personal Security

- ❖ Be alert to your surroundings, particularly in busy areas.
- ❖ Use well-lit, crowded locations, especially at night.

Transport Safety

- ❖ Choose licensed and reliable transportation services.
- ❖ Use seat belts and follow traffic restrictions.

Emergency Preparedness

- ❖ Ensure emergency contact numbers are easily available.
- ❖ Know the location of nearby hospitals and police stations.

Health and hygiene practices

Vaccinations & Travel Health

- ❖ Ensure all regular vaccines are up to date.
- ❖ Ask healthcare specialists for region-specific health advice.

Food and Water Safety

- ❖ Use dependable food sources and cook properly.
- ❖ Use bottled or filtered water, and avoid ice from unknown sources.

Mosquito-borne diseases

- ❖ Use insect repellent and wear long sleeves to prevent mosquito bites.
- ❖ Consider using mosquito netting in rooms without screened windows.

Environmental Safety

Sun Protection

- ❖ Use high-SPF sunscreen and reapply as necessary.
- ❖ Use protective clothes, caps, and sunglasses in direct sunlight.

Natural hazards

- ❖ Be aware of environmental hazards like uneven terrain, slick surfaces, and animals.
- ❖ Follow safety requirements while outside activities.

Cultural Awareness

Respect local customs.

- ❖ Become familiar with Jamaican customs and traditions.

- Wear suitable attire while visiting religious or cultural places.

Social Etiquette

- Demonstrate courtesy and consideration in your dealings.
- Avoid sensitive and confrontational talks.

Adopting safe and healthy behaviors allows you to experience Jamaica's beauty and culture more fully. Following these precise rules will guarantee a safe and rewarding trip on this intriguing island.

Emergency Information

Understanding emergency information and preparation procedures is critical for both homeowners and tourists. This detailed resource covers major elements of emergency circumstances in Jamaica.

Emergency services

Jamaica's emergency services are administered by the Jamaica Constabulary Force (JCF) and the Jamaica Fire Brigade. Dial 119 will contact the police, and 110 will contact the fire department. Emergency Medical Services (EMS) may be reached at 911.

Natural disasters

Hurricanes, earthquakes, and floods are all potential hazards in Jamaica. The hurricane season lasts from June to November. The Office of Disaster Preparedness and Emergency Management (ODPEM) is the national disaster management agency.

- ❖ Monitor weather updates throughout hurricane season. Follow evacuation instructions and have a storm pack ready.
- ❖ Earthquakes: Although Jamaica sits in a seismically active zone, large earthquakes are rare. Familiarize yourself with evacuation routes and do earthquake exercises.
- ❖ Floods: Heavy rains might cause floods. Stay updated on weather predictions, particularly during the rainy season.

Health emergencies

In the case of a health crisis, the Ministry of Health and Wellness takes center stage. To report a medical emergency, dial 911. Look for travel cautions and health warnings, particularly during illness outbreaks.

Transport and Road Safety

Road accidents might occur, so be careful. The JCF's Traffic Division handles road safety. Call 119 to promptly report an accident to the police. Learn the local traffic regulations and drive cautiously.

Tourism Assistance

The Tourism Product Development Company (TPDCo) assists travelers. If you experience any problems, call the TPDCo's emergency hotline at 1-888-776-4377.

Embassy and Consulate Information

Foreign nationals must know the location and contact information for their embassy or consulate in Jamaica. These diplomatic outposts may help during crises like natural catastrophes or legal concerns.

Communication

Keep up with local media, radio, and official government announcements. Follow the appropriate authorities' social media platforms to get real-time information.

Emergency Preparedness

Preparation is crucial. Make a family emergency plan, know where shelters are, and assemble an emergency pack with basics like water, non-perishable food, prescriptions, and critical papers.

Navigating crises in Jamaica requires being well-informed and prepared. Stay cautious, follow official instructions, and work with local authorities to safeguard your and others' safety during a crisis.

Currency and Money Matters

Currency

The Jamaican dollar (JMD)

- ❖ Jamaica's official currency is the Jamaican Dollar (JMD), represented by the sign "$" or "J$."
- ❖ The Bank of Jamaica regulates the issue and circulation of the Jamaican currency, which has undergone many alterations since its establishment.

Bank Notes and Coins

- ❖ Banknotes come in five denominations: $50, $100, $500, $1000, and $5000.
- ❖ Coins come in denominations of $1, $5, $10, and $20.

Monetary Policy and Regulation

Bank of Jamaica (BoJ)

- ❖ The Bank of Jamaica is the central bank, issuing and controlling the country's currency.
- ❖ The key goals are to preserve price stability, ensure financial system stability, and promote economic growth.

Exchange Rate Regime

Jamaica has a floating exchange rate system, allowing market forces to decide the value of the Jamaican dollar.

Inflation, interest rates, and foreign trade balances impact the currency rate.

Financial institutions

Commercial Banks

Jamaica has a strong banking industry with commercial banks, including the National Commercial Bank (NCB) and Scotiabank Jamaica.

These banks provide various services, such as savings accounts, loans, and electronic banking.

Credit unions

Credit unions are crucial in Jamaica's financial environment, offering financial services and promoting community-based solutions.

Microfinance institutions

Microfinance institutions help increase financial inclusion by providing modest loans and services to entrepreneurs and small companies.

Economic Challenges and Measures

Inflation

The Jamaican government and Bank of Jamaica limit inflation to protect the Jamaican Dollar's buying value.

Public Debt

Jamaica has encountered issues due to high levels of governmental debt. Efforts to control and decrease debt include fiscal discipline and economic changes.

Financial Inclusion

Initiatives aim to increase financial inclusion, giving more people access to banking and financial services.

Jamaica's currency and financial issues relate to its economic progress and stability. The Bank of Jamaica's involvement in currency regulation, along with a varied variety of financial institutions, adds to Jamaica's dynamic and ever-changing financial environment. Continued efforts to solve economic difficulties and increase financial inclusion will help shape Jamaica's financial destiny.

Basic Jamaican Patois Phrases

Many Jamaicans speak Jamaican Patois, often called Jamaican Creole, a colorful and expressive language. Here are 30 common Jamaican patois words that visitors could find useful:

Greetings

- "Wa gwan?" - What's happening? (How are you doing?)
- "Mi deh yah" means "I'm here."
- "Wah yuh deh pan?" means "What are you up to?" What are you doing?

General expressions

- "Mi deh yah" means "I'm here."

- The phrase "no problem" means "it's okay."
- "Likkle more" means "see you later" (a little time later).

Politeness

- "Tank yuh" means thank you.
- The phrase "Excuse mi" means "Excuse me."
- Use "Please" while requesting anything.

Getting around

- "How can I get to [destination]?"
- "Mi deh pon di road" means I'm on my way.
- "Di place deh deh so" refers to the location.

Food and drinks

- "Mi waan [food/drink]" means I want [food/drink].
- "Di food sweet" means the dish is tasty.
- The phrase "likkle more food" refers to a desire for more food.

Shopping

- "How much does this cost?" - What is the cost of this item?
- "Mi waan buy dat" means "I want to buy that."

Numbers

- "Wah di price?" - What's the price?
- "Mi haffi buy dat" means I have to buy it.

Time and Date

- "Wah time it deh?" - What time is it?
- "Mi deh yah fi [duration]" means "I'm here for [duration]."

Expressions of surprise

- "Cho!" - Oh, my!
- "Lawd!" - Oh, Lord!

Friendly Phrases

- "Mi deh yah fi likkle vibes" - I'm here for some fun.
- Use the phrase "Big up yuhself" to acknowledge and honor oneself (Greetings).

Weather

- "Di weather hot" means the weather is hot.
- "Mi love di breeze" means "I love the breeze."

Emergency phrases

- The phrase "Help mi!" means "Help me!"

- The phrase "Call di police!" means to call the police.

Remember that Jamaican Patois are varied, and pronunciation might vary. Locals enjoy tourists who attempt to speak their language, and these words may add a fun and genuine touch to your Jamaican trip!

Interacting with the locals.

Patois Language

While English is the official language, many Jamaicans speak Patois, a distinctive Jamaican creole. Engaging with people in Patois, even for a few words, may gain you respect and foster a more true relationship. Simple words like "Wah gwaan?" (What's up?) and "Mi deh yah" (I'm here) is well-received. I offered some Phrases earlier

Respect for the Elders

Respect for the elderly is firmly established in Jamaican society. When addressing seniors, use titles like "Mr.," "Mrs.," or "Miss" followed by their last name. When a senior enters the room, always stand to show respect.

Socialization and Small Talk

Jamaicans are noted for their friendliness and talkativeness. Engage in casual conversation, ask about their day, and demonstrate a genuine interest in the local culture. Family, sports, and music discussions are popular and may be effective icebreakers.

Invitations and hospitality

If welcomed to a Jamaican house, offering a little gift, such as flowers or a local delicacy is usual. Avoid coming too early or too late. Jamaicans are famed for their hospitality; therefore, receiving food or drink is a sign of gratitude.

Dress Code

Jamaicans are often proud of their looks and enjoy it when tourists show the same respect. Modest and immaculate clothes are recommended, particularly while visiting religious locations or rural regions.

Reggae Music and Dance

Music is an important component of Jamaican culture, with reggae being the most recognized genre. Do not be afraid to engage in the beat and dance during social occasions. It's an excellent method to break the ice and engage with locals on a deeper level.

Religious Sensitivity

Jamaica is a religiously diverse nation, with Christianity being the most common religion. Respect local norms and traditions, especially in religious settings. It's best to dress conservatively while visiting churches.

Interacting with residents in Jamaica is a joyful and rewarding experience that connects visitors with the island's heart and soul. Respecting cultural conventions, participating in cordial discussions, and enjoying the friendliness of the people will allow you to make lasting memories and true friendships on this lovely Caribbean island.

Photography Tips

Understand the light

- ❖ Take use of Jamaica's warm temperature and plentiful sunshine by shooting during the golden hours (early morning and late afternoon). The gentle, golden light highlights the colours and textures of your subjects.

- Utilize shadows and contrast to create unique effects. From lush woods to white sandy beaches, Jamaica's surroundings provide several possibilities to play with light and shadow.

Explore the local culture

Photograph street scenes in Kingston or Montego Bay to portray Jamaican culture. To respect local privacy and cultural traditions, engage with them, and ask for permission before shooting photographs.

Scenic landscapes

Jamaica's natural treasures include Dunn's River Falls and the Blue Mountains. Use a wide-angle lens to capture the majesty of magnificent settings, highlighting the size and beauty of the surroundings.

Wildlife Photography

- Bird Watching: Jamaica has a diversified bird population. Bring a zoom lens to capture the beautiful hues of hummingbirds or the magnificent flight of our national bird, the Doctor Bird (Swallow-Tail Hummingbird).
- Explore underwater life with waterproof camera gear, particularly in protected areas like Montego Bay Marine Park.

Candid Portraits

Capture Jamaican people's genuine expressions via local faces. Visit community events, festivals, and neighbourhood gatherings to capture the population's variety. Remember to establish rapport before capturing candid images.

Use of Colors

Jamaican culture is noted for its bright colors. Embrace this in your photographs by utilizing a diverse color scheme. Traditional dress, street art, and natural landscapes provide opportunities for visually striking and dynamic compositions.

Weather Considerations

Be prepared for unexpected rain showers, particularly during hurricane season. Bring some waterproof clothing to safeguard your equipment. Alternatively, utilize the rain creatively in your photographs.

Local Architecture

Visit historic sites such as Falmouth or Spanish Town to learn about colonial architecture. Use various angles and viewpoints to emphasize the delicate intricacies of old structures.

Night Photography

Capture the nightlife in places like Kingston and Ocho Rios. Experiment with long-exposure images to capture the energy and brightness of the urban environment.

Respect the environment.

Leave No Trace: Be conscious of your surroundings, particularly in nature. Practice responsible travel by leaving the environment as you found it. When shooting images, respect local conventions and restrictions.

With its rich cultural tapestry and different scenery, Jamaica becomes an enticing canvas for photographers. Understanding the intricacies of light, culture, and the environment allows you to create a visual story that highlights Jamaica's beauty and respects and celebrates its people and legacy. Happy shooting!

Travel Apps

These applications may improve your trip experience by offering crucial information, navigation aids, and access to local services.

Visit Jamaica Official App

Jamaica's official tourist app provides a complete reference of sights, lodgings, and activities.

Key features

- ❖ Provide tourist information and guides.
- ❖ Local festivals and event calendars.
- ❖ Maps and navigation features.
- ❖ Provide emergency contact information.

Google Maps

This navigation software helps find routes, explore local businesses, and discovering nearby activities.

Key features

- ❖ Detailed maps using satellite imagery.
- ❖ Get real-time traffic information.
- ❖ Restaurant reviews and ratings.
- ❖ Provide offline maps for places with inadequate connection.

XE Currency Converter

A helpful program for changing currencies, particularly for managing travel spending.

Key features

- ❖ Current currency exchange rates.
- ❖ Use historical charts for reference.
- ❖ Offline mode allows for usage without an internet connection.

Weather Underground

This app gives accurate and up-to-date weather predictions for Jamaica.

Key features

- ❖ Provide hourly and 10-day predictions.
- ❖ Interactive radar and satellite maps.
- ❖ Receive severe weather notifications.

Uber or Lyft?

Uber and Lyft provide ridesharing services in Jamaica, making them handy alternatives to conventional taxis.

Key features

- ❖ Ensures safe and dependable conveyance.
- ❖ Cashless transactions.
- ❖ Get real-time tracking of your ride.

Jamaica Yellow Pages

This software provides a database of local businesses in Jamaica, including services, restaurants, and facilities.

Key features

- ❖ Search for companies by name or category.
- ❖ Contact details and reviews.
- ❖ Maps provide directions.

WhatsApp

WhatsApp is a popular communication tool in Jamaica. It may help you remain in contact with locals, other tourists, and tour guides.

Key features

- ❖ Supports messaging, audio, and video calls.
- ❖ Share your location in real-time.
- ❖ Use group conversations for coordination.

JUTC (Jamaican Urban Transit Company

The JUTC app offers bus routes and timetables in Jamaica, making it useful for anyone using public transit.

Key features

- ❖ Provide bus timetables and routes.
- ❖ Receive real-time information on bus whereabouts.
- ❖ Fare information.

Jamaica Customs Traveler

This app informs foreign tourists about customs procedures and requirements when entering Jamaica.

Key features

- ❖ Understanding customs rules and allowances.
- ❖ FAQs for typical traveler inquiries.
- ❖ Contact details for customs offices.

Remember to download these applications before your travel to access offline capabilities and prevent network concerns. Stay up to speed on the newest travel warnings and app versions to have the best possible experience in Jamaica. Safe travels!

Time Zone

Understanding Jamaica's time zone is critical for effective communication, scheduling, and collaboration with people and enterprises worldwide.

Jamaica uses Eastern Standard Time (EST) throughout the year. However, it's worth noting that Jamaica does not follow Daylight Saving Time (DST). This implies that the time in Jamaica stays consistent, eliminating the need to move clocks forward or backward during DST shifts. Consequently, the time difference between Jamaica and places that use DST may change throughout the year.

UTC Offset: Jamaica's regular time is five hours behind Coordinated Universal Time. This stable time offset provides consistency for residents and tourists in managing their everyday routines and international interactions.

Impact on Communication: Understanding time zones is critical for communicating effectively with people and companies all around the globe. Jamaica is on Eastern Standard Time, which means it shares a time zone with the eastern United States and portions of Canada during the standard period.

Corporate and International Relations: Jamaica's time zone is well-positioned for corporate relations with North American and

European peers. The continuous time zone without DST modifications makes scheduling and coordinating meetings, conference calls, and other collaborative initiatives easier, resulting in more effective worldwide company operations.

Tourism Considerations: Tourists visiting Jamaica should consider the time zone while booking activities, flights, and lodgings. Furthermore, recognizing the time difference between Jamaica and their home nation allows passengers to quickly acclimate to local time and minimize schedule delays.

Daylight Saving Time (DST) Observance: Unlike many other nations that alternate between normal time and DST, Jamaica maintains a constant time standard without using DST. This simplifies timekeeping for people and companies, removing the need for biannual adjustments and any misunderstanding caused by DST shifts.

Jamaica's time zone, which follows Eastern Standard Time but does not observe Daylight Saving Time, is critical to the island's international connections. Understanding Jamaica's time zone is critical for smooth communication with the rest of the globe, whether for business, tourism, or general purposes. The stable time zone, a fundamental part of everyday life, symbolizes Jamaica's dedication to simplicity and efficiency in its connection with the global world.

Conclusion

As we conclude our holistic travel guide to Jamaica, we genuinely hope that our adventure has stirred your wanderlust and inspired you to experience the incomparable charm of this Caribbean treasure. Jamaica, with its rhythmic rhythms, kind hospitality, and stunning surroundings, invites you to have unforgettable experiences on your next holiday.

A Tapestry of Experiences: Jamaica is more than just a destination; it is a tapestry of experiences ready to be woven into your travel narrative. From the mystical Blue Mountains to Kingston's colorful markets and Negril's sun-kissed beaches, every area of this island country has distinct character and promises remarkable experiences.

Reggae Rhythms and Warm Smiles: Feel the island's heartbeat while immersing yourself in the enticing rhythms of reggae music. Allow the sounds to carry you through colorful street celebrations, where residents dance exuberantly, greeting you with warm grins and open hearts. The soul of Jamaica is as much about the people as it is about the breathtaking scenery.

Culinary Delights to Savor: Indulge your taste buds in a symphony of flavors that distinguish Jamaican food. Each dish reflects diverse culinary traditions, from jerk chicken to ackee and saltfish.

Participate in the local cuisine scene, where roadside kiosks and gourmet restaurants provide a culinary experience representing the island's many cultural influences.

Island Adventures & Water Wonders: Jamaica offers a canvas of adventure for adrenaline seekers and nature lovers alike. Explore secret waterfalls, dive into crystal-clear seas filled with marine life, and hike through the island's verdant interior. Jamaica welcomes you to explore its natural beauties, whether zip-lining through the trees or relaxing on a bamboo raft along the Martha Brae River.

Explore Jamaica's rich history and culture, which help create its identity. Visit the ancient Rose Hall Great House, follow Bob Marley's footsteps at Nine Mile, and visit the UNESCO-listed Maroon heritage sites. Each cultural interaction reveals layers of a story that has created the strong and lively character of the Jamaican people.

Choosing Jamaica: A Choice for the Heart: As you plan your next trip, think about Jamaica as more than simply a location on a map. Whether you want leisure on the beautiful beaches, adventure in the lush rainforests, or connection via cultural inquiry, Jamaica has many activities to satisfy any traveler's spirit.

Jamaica is more than a holiday destination; it is an invitation to experience life in its purest and most colorful form. Allow the island's personality to fascinate you, its people to inspire you, and its vistas to make a lasting impression on your trip memories. Your Jamaican adventure awaits you; prepare to explore, learn, and make memories that will last a lifetime. Until then, One Love, One Heart, let's come together and feel good in the country of wood and water, Jamaica!

Bonus: Travel Budget Planner & Travel Journal

TRAVEL BUDGET PLANNER

DESTINATION: _____   TRAVEL DATES: _____

TRANSPORTATION | BUDGETED | ACTUAL

	BUDGETED	ACTUAL
AIRFARE	$ _____	$ _____
AIRPORT PARKING	$ _____	$ _____
CHECKED LUGGAGE	$ _____	$ _____
CAR RENTAL	$ _____	$ _____
BUS / TAXI / TRANSIT / TRAIN	$ _____	$ _____
TOTAL	$ _____	$ _____

ACCOMMODATION

	BUDGETED	ACTUAL
HOTEL/ AIR BNB	$ _____	$ _____
PARKING	$ _____	$ _____
MISCELLANEOUS COSTS	$ _____	$ _____
TOTAL	$ _____	$ _____

FOOD & DRINK

	BUDGETED	ACTUAL
RESTAURANTS	$ _____	$ _____
SNACKS	$ _____	$ _____
COFFEE & TEA	$ _____	$ _____
GROCERIES	$ _____	$ _____
TOTAL	$ _____	$ _____

ENTERTAINMENT

	BUDGETED	ACTUAL
ORGANIZED TOURS	$ _____	$ _____
SIGHTSEEING & ATTRACTIONS	$ _____	$ _____
NIGHTLIFE	$ _____	$ _____
SPA TREATMENTS	$ _____	$ _____
SHOPPING	$ _____	$ _____
MISCELLANEOUS	$ _____	$ _____
TOTAL	$ _____	$ _____

OTHER EXPENSES

	BUDGETED	ACTUAL
TRAVEL INSURANCE	$ _____	$ _____
PASSPORT, VISA, DOCUMENTS	$ _____	$ _____
VACCINATIONS & MEDICATIONS	$ _____	$ _____
MOBILE PHONE FEES	$ _____	$ _____
CURRENCY EXCHANGE	$ _____	$ _____
MISCELLANEOUS COSTS	$ _____	$ _____
TOTAL	$ _____	$ _____
GRAND TOTAL	$ _____	$ _____

TRAVEL

DATE:

DURATION:

DESTINATION:

PLACES TO SEE:	LOCAL FOOD TO TRY:
1.	1.
2.	2.
3.	3.
4.	4.
5.	5.
6.	6.
7.	7.

DAY 1

DAY 2

DAY 3

DAY 4

DAY 5

DAY 6

NOTES

EXPENSES IN TOTAL:

PLANNER

TRAVEL

DATE:
DURATION:

DESTINATION:

PLACES TO SEE:
1.
2.
3.
4.
5.
6.
7.

LOCAL FOOD TO TRY:
1.
2.
3.
4.
5.
6.
7.

DAY 1

DAY 2

DAY 3

DAY 4

DAY 5

DAY 6

NOTES

EXPENSES IN TOTAL:

PLANNER

TRAVEL

DATE:

DURATION:

DESTINATION:

PLACES TO SEE:
1. _____
2. _____
3. _____
4. _____
5. _____
6. _____
7. _____

LOCAL FOOD TO TRY:
1. _____
2. _____
3. _____
4. _____
5. _____
6. _____
7. _____

DAY 1	DAY 2	DAY 3

DAY 4	DAY 5	DAY 6

NOTES

EXPENSES IN TOTAL:

PLANNER

Notes

Notes

Notes

Notes

Printed in Great Britain
by Amazon

8dae640d-826e-40fe-ba49-322eceb8e1a0R01